DORINDA'S
BIRTHDAY
A CORNISH IDYLL

BY CHARLES LEE
AUTHOR OF "THE
WIDOW WOMAN," "A
FOREIGNER IN PEN-
DENNACK," AND OTHER
STORIES

NEW YORK
E. P. DUTTON & CO.

DORINDA'S BIRTHDAY

Dorinda puts up her hair

DORINDA PUTS UP HER HAIR

ADVICE TO THE READER

If you will needs be merry with your wits,
  Take heed of names and figuring of natures,
And tell how near the goose the gander sits,
  Of *Hal* and *Lil*, and of such silly creatures . . .
But scorn them not, for they are honest people,
Although perhaps they never saw Paul's steeple.

Nich. Breton.

DORINDA'S BIRTHDAY

I

Dorinda and some others dwelt at Sunny Corner, a little group of cottages situated in Nanheviock Valley, just above the sudden twist the road makes when it has left Porthmellan behind and is preparing to rush the hill which leads to St. Hender Churchtown. In happy Cornwall well-nigh every parish has its Sunny Corner—favoured spot where rough winds never venture and the mid-day sun shines in at the front windows; but of all Sunny Corners from Land's End to the Devon borders, Dorinda's home and birthplace is the prettiest and choicest to my mind. *Ille terrarum mihi praeter omnes angulus ridet.*

B   I

Here, you would say, Nature has decreed that life should go to a gay and trivial tune—the selfsame tune that the stream babbles as it curves a protecting arm about the spot. Your approach from the road is by way of a green wicket-gate, through a small orchard of old apple-trees, and over the stream by a plank bridge. Then you have before you a row of three white-washed, brown-thatched cottages. Fuchsias bloom by the doors without ; geraniums flatten their faces against the panes within. There is a wholesome smell of wood-smoke in the air, and through the tangle of bird-songs —nowhere do throstle and robin sing so sweetly and persistently—you hear now and again that most comfortable of natural sounds, the grunting of a well-fed pig. In one window you will observe an array of small groceries and haberdasheries—

tea, biscuits, tape, and the like. For all ordinary contingencies Sunny Corner is complete and self-contained, holding up its head in an attitude of independence, not untinged with scorn, of its bigger neighbours, the fishing village below and the churchtown above. The ladies of Sunny Corner were at a loss to imagine how people could endure to live in such rackety places, and they could moralize you excellently on the evils of town life with its all-too-frequent opportunities for gadding and scandalmongering, on the corrupting influence of bakehouses and the ruin of domestic happiness brought about by boughten bread, with its fell train of consequences—indigestion, ill-temper, henpecking, wife-beating, the workhouse and the jail.

The human population of Sunny Corner numbered nine all told, and it was sym-

metrically distributed among the three
houses, each of which contained two
seniors and a junior.   At the end house to
the left dwelt Mr. and Mrs. Barron with
their son Hubert, a steady young man of
five-and-twenty : at the end house to the
right, Lazarus Roscorla, his maiden sister
Philippa, and their orphaned nephew
Charles Edward, a hulking lad of fifteen ; while the middle house contained
the Varco family—father, mother, and
Dorinda.

The task—no easy one—of describing
my heroine, I can best approach obliquely,
by way of the stream which flows down
the valley past her window. It is a
fanciful, capricious little river, never of
the same mind for two moments together.
Now it loiters to nibble teasingly at its
patient banks, now it hurries round a
corner to see what wonders may be beyond ;

here it spins in a round, there it slides gurgling over a rocky shelf. It tips headlong into tiny disasters ; it chatters to the ferns and meadowsweet in a dozen contradictory voices at once ; it darts this way and that, like one of its own startled trout ; it dances up to the road, crooking a friendly elbow, and before the challenge can be accepted it is out of sight, hiding coquettishly among the willows. Or for a dozen yards it will play the great sober river, and sweep along without a ripple, bearing mighty twigs and straws away with resistless force. Then it approaches a two-foot weir ; you see the nymph with finger on lip, and eyes that twinkle with suppressed fun, and stealthy silent feet ; the tremendous leap is made, and for yards below the bubble and flash of riotous merriment continues. Birds linger by it, sing their loudest to it, swing their nests over it. Flowers crowd to its brink ; in spring, when the daffodils are out, it rolls a flood of innocent gold. Little springs, sudden fancies of the earth, gush from the rocky hill-side and trickle across the road to join it. It tastes pleasantly of moorland peat and water-mint.

Imagine its tutelary Naiad, and you have Dorinda. Do you wish me to be more definite ? Dorinda at seventeen was a straight, shapely, nut-brown maid, whose features were ever at play with one another and mostly at charming variance. Now the lips were shy, and the eyes shot laughter under demure brows ; now the timid eyes veiled themselves beneath your scrutiny, while the dispossessed laughter flitted to the lips, and the brows went up in scornful contradiction to inaccessible heights.

When Dorinda spoke, you heard a gay

6

thrush. When she laughed, it was the willow-wren, whose joyous song trips up the scale and down again in an effortless sweet warble and vanishes imperceptibly on the air. When she stood, she was like a young poplar, liveliest and most upright of rooted things. When she walked, you looked every moment to see her break into dancing. When she ran, you were reminded of those little shore-birds that hurry over the sands with twinkling feet.

For her character, let one fact speak, on the eve of her seventeenth birthday the first putting-up of her hair was still an event in the future. You may see nothing in this, but I assure you that it stamps her at once as somebody quite out of the common. At Porthmellan and St. Hender and all about, the maidens can scarcely await the final shelving of their school-books before taking the step that launches them irrevocably into womanhood. Even before that date, more than one packet of experimental hairpins will have been bought, and every known style of *coiffure* tried, abandoned, and reverted to again and again before the looking-glass. The next Sunday after the last breaking-up day is the latest date to which the impatient maiden will consent to defer her public appearance in waved or braided top-knot. But Dorinda's schooldays receded into the dim past, her skirts crept down and down to her ankles, and still the brown curls tossed unrestrained on her shoulders from Monday to Friday. Still on Saturday they underwent a day-long discipline of rags in front and tight little plaits behind, and still on Sunday she continued to look almost as pretty as ever in the midst of a frizzy halo that would have passed muster in New Guinea itself. Mocking com-

8

parisons to an owl looking out of an ivy-
bush left her unmoved ; and she never
blenched at the sight of her juniors by a
year walking out with wage-earners, while
she had to content herself with an unprofit-
able dalliance with boys.

But custom cannot be violated with
impunity. Dam up the most harmless of
streams, and at once it becomes a potential
danger to the community, and the date of
the breaking of the dam is fixed for ever
in the memory of mankind. So with the
putting up of Dorinda's hair.

The day on which the rite was per-
formed is calendared with three events :
for Sunny Corner it was Dorinda's
seventeenth birthday ; for the world at
large it was Midsummer Day ; for the
folk of Nanheviock Valley and thereabouts
it was St. Hender Feast Day, with sports
and games in the glebe-meadow and a

bell-ringing contest in the church tower. In this last event Sunny Corner had a special interest; for Nick Barron was organizer and fugleman of the home team, and Hubert its latest recruit, chosen only the previous week out of the junior team to fill the gap left by the retirement of a veteran, whose strength after sixty years was beginning at last to lag behind his skill and enthusiasm.

On Midsummer Day, then, our tale begins; the time, an hour or so after dinner; the place, Mrs. Varco's kitchen, with the folk of Sunny Corner assembled there in their best clothes. The Barrons, to be sure, are absent. Father and son have already departed for the field of tourney, and Mrs. Barron, an invalid of the most determined kind, remains in the upper chamber which she seldom quits. Dorinda, too, is still mysteriously occupied up-stairs ; but the others are all present.

The host is a little wiry man with the bright eyes and the alert demeanour of a cock-robin. Comparative strangers identify him by his flaming beard, which is no mere weak, drooping excrescence, as too many big beards are apt to be, but a great bristly bush that juts out, by far the most prominent feature in his physiognomy, like a thorn-clump on the face of a precipice. When he is smoking his favourite briar with the bent stem, the bowl of it nestles in the ruddy tangle like a pipkin in a brushwood fire, and every now and again a too vigorous puff diffuses a perceptible odour of singed hair about him. He is pacing the floor up and down, fisherman-fashion, five steps each way. Not that Dickon Varco is a fisherman, but the ceaseless ambling to

and fro of the man of nets and crab-pots
is congenial to his restless spirit, and he
adopts it as to the manner born. Plaster-
ing is his trade, and, in his own mock
modest phrase, he can whitewash a barn
door so well as any mason ; though his
true vocation, as is so often the case,
lies in a bypath, and the real business
and passion of his life is the cure and
care of clocks. Should a staid veteran
timepiece suddenly abandon it century-
long habits of sobriety, and race ahead
into to-morrow before to-day is over, or
should it despondently throw up the
sponge and refuse to go on counting the
interminable hours any longer, a message
to Dickon will always cause him to cast
down pail and brush and hurry post-haste
to bring it to its senses. No sale of
furniture is held within a circuit of
twelve miles, but Dickon is in attendance ;

and when the household clock comes under the hammer, the chances are that it passes into his possession after a characteristically breathless bidding-bout. Then, if it be of the race of Grandfathers, he balances himself with a weight in either pocket, wedges his back inside the case, and trots home, like a gigantic tortoise on its hind legs. The shock of meeting him thus caparisoned in dark lanes after nightfall has scattered many pairs of sauntering lovers in hasty flight.

Dickon is a seller as well as a buyer, and clocks come and go. Sometimes there will be only one in the house, sometimes half a dozen. At present he possesses four : two in the kitchen, grandsires both, the one a " flowery-face," the other of brazen visage ; one in the parlour, a brisk, light-hearted cuckoo, that counts no dark days and has no

13

winter in its year, but even in the smallest hours of the darkest January night declares unhesitatingly for a May morning and bright sunshine; and one on the landing upstairs. This last is no sober Briton, but a foreigner whose incurably dissolute habits cause Dickon much anxiety. From the Black Forest it comes, and holds heterodox—presumably papistical—views on the subject of time. It is for ever chiming wrong hours in a shrill insistent treble, and, when permitted, plays frivolous waltzes *prestissimo* on a concealed barrel-organ.

At one end of the aged horsehair sofa under the window sits Dickon's wife Thomasine, a large, round, kindly dame without a prickle or angle in her structure. Destiny manifestly framed her in a comfortable mould for a leisurely progress through life, and then, after Destiny's

14

seemingly perverse fashion, linked her to an embodiment of bustle. But in this case at any rate Destiny knew what it was about, and never made a more suitable match. Conceive the average housewife of normal irritability in Mrs. Varco's shoes, cursed with the dismal certainty of always knowing the time, of having to stare her in the face wherever she looked, of never being able to forget it and float into an eternity of oblivious musing. Think of it—all those tall grim onlookers inexorably measuring every trivial little business, every momentary lapse into idleness! The slow ticking of a single timepiece grows to be part of the silence of a well-ordered house ; you heed it no more than you do the beating of your own heart. But several together !—oh, the tread of multitudinous feet, hurrying you with them in their mad rush down the steep slope of years ! Time is hastening so fast that his minions cannot keep step. One clock can be managed and cajoled ; you can put it back when dinner is behind-hand and a hungry husband is at the gate ; you can put it forward when you thirst for a comforting cup and tea-time lags. But the most hardened domestic conscience would hesitate to tamper with four or five witnesses at once. I have no statistics at hand to show how many watchmakers' wives end their days in lunatic asylums, but surely the percentage must be a large one. Fortunately Mrs. Varco is blessed with a temperament that nothing can ruffle or hurry. Time writes no wrinkles on her placid brow, and she is far too stout to run races with him. About her, stationary for the most part in her kitchen, the little world of Sunny Corner revolves ; from her ample store of good-will the soothing oil flows forth at the faintest squeak in the social machinery.

At the other end—the bolstered end—of the sofa sits Miss Roscorla. Politeness —not to be forgone even among inti-mates—has offered her the seat which is fondly supposed to be the most comfort-able in the room, and politeness has com-pelled her acceptance of it, though she had far rather be elsewhere ; partly be-cause, being thin and angular, she has an ancient feud with the bolster, which is indeed a most uncompromising bolster, and partly because, whenever her hostess is seized with a paroxysm of laughter (which happens to that worthy soul at least once a minute), the vibrations com-municate themselves to the sofa's few remaining springs, and boggle her up, as she complains to herself, like a farm cart going over a turnip field. Miss Roscorla's own interior mechanism would appear to be constructed entirely of springs and wires. As she sits bolt upright with folded arms, her stillness is the unnatural stillness of a clockwork toy, wound up but not yet set a-going ; a touch somewhere, and the thin tight lips will snap apart, the hands will be suddenly released from their fast clutch of the elbows, and there is no way known to mortals of arresting the motion of either until the works run down of their own accord. On her head she wears a grey sailor hat, severely unadorned save for one ancient feather, stripped of most of its plumes, set at an angle nearly approaching the vertical, and resembling nothing so much as a quill pen in an old-fashioned leaden inkstand.

Mr. Roscorla is jammed against the wall with a guardian timepiece at either

elbow, like a prisoner between two senti-
nel policemen. His blank brown face,
encircled with a fringe of grizzled hair,
may be likened, for colour and expressive-
ness of feature, to a ploughed field within
a fence of flowering blackthorn. His soft
black hat is on his head, and in his hand
he carries a stout and curiously knotted
stick, with which he collogues from time
to time as with a familiar spirit, applying
its knob now to his lips, now to one of
his ears, now to the orbit of either eye.

Lastly, Charles Edward lolls and fidgets
by himself in a remote corner. Every few
moments he glances anxiously at one of
the clocks, and then at the door. His
bosom is a skirmishing ground of con-
tending passions. Pleasure bids him break
loose from his dawdling elders and hasten
to join the revelling crowd; Love whispers
him to endure their tedious talk a little

longer, that he may be rewarded with Dorinda's company going up the hill. Why lingers she, and what will she think when she sees him in a stand-up collar ?

We are to strike into the conversation immediately on the heels of old Time, who with much senile wheezing and clucking has just proclaimed the hour of Three in two loud voices of equal emphasis but varying pitch. Blithe corroboration came immediately in muffled tones from spring's harbinger in the next room. A pause, and then a thin hurried voice from up-stairs gave the others the lie direct, querulously declaring that Five was the true reckoning.

" The foreigner's off ahead agin," remarked Mr. Varco. " And marking twenty past one this very minute, I'll be bound. Like a maid, saying one thing, looking another, and maning something

quite deffrant all the while. And spaking
of maids—Dorinda-a ! Three o'clo-ock !' "

"Coming, father !" trilled a skylark
from on high—if you can imagine a skylark with its beak full of hairpins.

"Come, then. What's up with the
maid ? She don't use to be so long over
her trumpery."

Mr. Roscorla got on the track of an
idea. Warily hunting it down, he shifted
the knob of his stick from his mouth,
brought it delicately round by the bridge
of his nose and over the arch of his right
eyebrow, and there ran his quarry to
earth.

"Husband-high, neighbour," he said, in
a voice that creaked as if rusty from
disuse. "And when a maiden's husband-
high, d'ye see——"

"Tshutt !" Mr. Varco caught the
application on the wing, and tossed it

contemptuously aside. "Tshutt! Our li'll maid husband-high! Nonsense! She've no age in her at all!"

"She'll be well on for seventeen, though, I should say," remarked Miss Roscorla.

"Seventeen's her age this very day," said Mrs. Varco. "Dickon have a quip about that. What's your quip, master, about Dorinda's birthday being Midsummer Day?"

"High tide o' the year; that's the time to launch your craft 'pon the waters of life. I made that quip the very hour the cheeld was born. A nate li'll quip, sure 'nough," said the author impersonally.

"'Tis so, sure," agreed Miss Roscorla graciously. "D'st hear that, Lazarus? Midsummer Day—that's high tide, like; and high tide's the time to launch your craft—see? Kind of a parable, Lazarus, like the maid was a skiffie-boat."

Mr. Roscorla transferred the knob to the other eyebrow, found no enlightenment there, tapped his forehead with no better success, propped his hat up an inch or two, as if to give his brain more room, failed again, and returned with evident relief to his original branch of the subject.

" Husband-high, I was saying. Seventeen's husband-high, 'a b'lieve."

" Courtship-high, anyway," said Miss Varco, with a sigh and a laugh.

" Same thing nowadays," said Miss Roscorla. " The ondacent hurry of these maids——"

" 'Nother quip!" exclaimed Mr. Varco. " 'Tis like the rat. ' Master,' says the clown, ' do 'e know 'bout the rat ?' ' No, sir, I do not know 'bout the rat,' says the man with the whip. ' Master,' says the clown, with his hands in his pockets, a-waggling of his trowses, ' master,' says

23

he 'the rat that got the longest tail do take the longest time to get inside the trap.' And then smack go the whip and round go the specketty horse with the young lady 'pon top. And so for these maids. Seventeen, very well ; twenty, not so bad ; but after that the tail of years do lengthen like a clothes-line, and the longer 'tis, the harder 'tis to get inside church door with a man on your arm. But our maid don't seem in no ondacent hurry. Dorinda-a ! "

" In a minute, daddy ! "

" In a minute ! We d' all know the maning of that in the mouth of a she. Fine pretty job 'a 'd be if the women had the making of the clocks. We'd be landed in Etarnity by next week, I reckon. Well, friends, be us to wait for the maid, or ben't us ? The band 'll have pitched playing this hour and more, and the ring-

ing 'll all be over before we get up-along
if we don't hurry."

"Aw, gie the maid time," said Miss
Roscorla. "I ben't in no vi'lence for the
hooting and tooting of the one, nor yet
for the clashing and dashing of the other.
I don't hold with this ringing like 'tis
nowadays, in and out, forth and back, till
your brain's all of a maze trying to
follow. Down the gamut stiddy for half-
an-hour 'pon end—that's how 'a used to
be in my young days, and none of this
low deceitful dodgery. And such carnal
music as these bands do play—dances and
ballats and marble halls—'tidn' fit for a
saved person to listen to. Well, what is
'a, Lazarus? Spake up, before your hat
do fall off."

Her sisterly eye had detected symptoms
of a renewed ferment in Mr. Roscorla's
brain. His stick, ploughing its cautious

way through his scanty locks, was pushing his hat back and back into the position of an angelic halo. Now, slowly retracing its path, it came to rest between nose and upper lip, where its magic touch unsealed the fountain of speech.

"Spaking of these circuses, neighbour. I went to a circus myself once. When I was a frolicsome young spark, 'twas. See a helephant having his dinner. Ringed a bell, 'a did. Man brought en a cabbage. Elephant clunked en down like a brussel-sprout. Ringed the bell again. 'Nother cabbage. Clunked that down. Bell agin. If you'll believe me, *'nother* cabbage. Satisfied? Not he! Bell once more. *'Nother* cab——"

"That'll do, Lazarus," said his sister sharply; and Mr. Roscorla, who had become positively animated under the influence of his exciting narrative, was

26

suddenly and completely checked, remaining with mouth wide open and stick feebly groping in mid-air, while Miss Roscorla proceeded to excuse and explain her summary action.

"There's nine cabbages come into that yarn, Mis' Varco, and if I don't stop him he give the whole pedigree of 'em from first to last, till I'm ready to jump out of my skin. 'Tis the only yarn he've got, you see, and he don't often get a chance to tell en, only at a particular time, once in three year or so ; so you can't blame the poor soul for making the most of en, can 'e ? Shut your mouth, Lazarus, before the draught do get to that holler tooth o' yourn."

"Capital yarn too," said Dickon, extending the professional's kindly patronage to the bungling amateur. "But malincholy. To think of all that appetite

27

wasted 'pon raw vege'bles ! Looksee now, friends, we'll gie the maid two minutes more, and if she don't come by then———"

" Here she is at last, I do believe ! "

A light winnowing sound was heard, as of the wings of wrens and titmice ; the door was wafted abroad, and Dorinda stood before her friends and relatives.

II

By all the rules that govern a heroine's
first appearance, she should have been
wearing a dress of some soft clinging
material, half hiding and half revealing
the gracious curves of her figure, and
foamed over by vaporous billows of filmy
chiffon. But if the truth must out,
Dorinda's white muslin dress was as stiff
as starch could make it, and there was
nothing vague or ambiguous about the
primly ordered rows of pink trimming
that adorned it. Here was no confused
flow of ribands, no sweet disorder of
erring lace or tempestuous petticoat, but
from the white hat to the white shoes
and stockings, all was taut and trim.
The excitement of the moment had

slightly disturbed her breathing ; and
with each soft pant a mysterious inward
cheeping was audible, as though, like
Lesbia, she cherished a happy sparrow
in her bosom. Her slim throat was
chained and clamped with several bead
necklaces, and more than one brooch
of genuine rolled gold ; and I am very
much afraid that the slight ridge or
swelling which was defined on one of
her fingers under the white glove was
attributable to a sixpenny diamond ring.
Yet how bravely she carried her bravery !
how alive, how irrepressibly flexible she
contrived to appear under it all ! like—if
I may drag a simile from afar—like a
folk-song, which some eminently respectable musician has tricked out and bur-
dened down with conventional harmonies
and *rococo* cadences.

Little conscious smiles played about

her face. For a moment silence reigned; then Mr. Varco began.

"Young woman, where's my little daughter Dorinda? And who be you, with your fine fligs so gay?"

"Father!" she twittered, struggling to compose her triumphant laughter.

Mr. Varco went through a condensed drama of recognition, peering, frowning, starting.

"No! Yes! No, but 'a can't be! Yes, but 'a must be! Missus, this young lady's our Dorinda. My life!" He sank exhausted in a chair. "Bit all-overish; better direckly. Like one of these story-books: long-lost cheeld come back to her sorrowing parents, that grand and growed up, they don't know her. And the young dook hiding in the back-kitchen this very minute, waiting for to claim his bride! Well, well! Fotch out the young dook,

31

and down 'pon your hands and knees the two of 'e, till I give 'e my blessing. Fotch en out, I say!"

She shook her head and sighed.

" How! Don't tell me you've been and took up with that there barrinet with the black mushtash! Don't 'e, my cheeld. He've a wife up to the asylum already, beside the one he sticked with the carving-knife last week because the mutton was underdone, and her life-blood did flow like gravy 'pon the clane table-cloth. Aw, don't tell me 'tis the barrinet!"

" Do give over with your nonsense, Dickon!" cried Mrs. Varco, her fat sides shaking.

Mr. Varco held up his hand.

" Wait a bit. I have en. 'Tis the young squire. Bit of a come-down after the dook, but you might ha' done worse. A galliant blade, the young squire; and

32

what's all the pomps of the earth, put 'em agin a happy home ? The dook's mother's a' old cat, if you ask me. She and the missus 'ud never get along together, I seem."

" Dickon !" protested the rolling, gasping missus. " 'Tidn' fitty to put such notions in the cheeld's head."

" Ay, but they'm there already, trust her else. Come, you maid, who's the chap ? "

Again she heaved a mock sigh.

" Aw, don't tell me there an't no young feller somewheres around !"

" 'Tis the terrible truth," murmured she. " And I'm awful kind to them too."

" Poor li'll maid ! Well, must see what we can do for 'e." He revolved a deeply speculative eye, and fastened it on Mr. Roscorla. " Ah, here's the very one !

D 33

Staid bachelor man with a bit of property.
Not so young as 'a was, but sound in
wind and limb, not a hounce of vice into
'm, straight as a willow, gentle as a dove.
Cast your eye upon 'm."

With inconceivable slowness Mr. Roscorla's features stiffened into alarmed
bewilderment, relaxed into an uneasy
smile, and finally twisted themselves into
an awesome grimace, which, with a
little good-will, might pass current for
an amorous smirk.

"There!" exclaimed Mr. Varco. "See
how loving 'a do look upon 'e! Haven'
'e something to say to 'm, now?"

"'Tis for the man to speak and the
maid to listen," said Dorinda.

"Hear that! She d' know the rules
already, and her hair not put up ten
minutes. Who've ben larning her the
rules, I'd like to know? Well, come,

uncle, the maid's a-waiting. Don't mind we. Pitch and begin your courting."

Miss Roscorla began to stir and snort, while her brother consulted his oracular staff. His blank visage brightened by infinite gradations, as brightens the eastern sky at dawn, and he spoke.

" Fine growing weather for the craps," said he.

" Not so bad to begin with," remarked Mr. Varco. " Can't do better 'n start with the weather. 'Tis like the first move 'pon the chequer-board—always the same, whether you'm playing for love or for money. Now 'tis the maiden's turn. The rule is for the maiden to turn it off with a quip. Out with your quip, Dorinda."

" Fine courting weather for the chaps," said Dorinda with a giggle. Please to understand : you are not to judge her, here or elsewhere, by your sophisticated drawing-room standards. No doubt a countess in a like situation could have turned the repartee differently and refined on the giggle. But Dorinda is no countess, and the realist refrains from importing into a humble cottage the icy manners and lambent wit of the gilded saloon. Her paternal critic was satisfied ; let his criterion be yours for the time.

"Very well," he said approvingly. "Straight to the pint, and leave the chap to jedge whether you'm stroking his face or slapping of it. Now, uncle, your move. Something gay but tender, and more meant than do meet the eye."

But Miss Roscorla's disapproval of this dangerous trifling now rose to the point where it could no longer be suppressed.

"A joke's a joke," she said, jumping to her feet. "I'm all for a joke myself,

36

when *'tis* a joke ; but not when it turn to tejousness, making a mock of grey hairs and putting fullish notions into empty heads. Come, Lazarus."

In the circles to which I address my tale, the art of winking is rapidly falling into desuetude. More's the pity. In all the silent language of the eye, there is no more expressive vocable, when enunciated by a skilled practitioner like Mr. Varco.

Miss Roscorla led the way with her brother, grasping him firmly by the arm, while with her disengaged hand she adjusted his hat, arranged his neckcloth, and felt in his various pockets to make sure that handkerchief, pipe, pouch and money were in their proper places. Behind them Dickon towed his wife to the door, where he remembered a neglected duty and darted off " to mait the pegs," leaving

her to waddle on alone. Dorinda lingered,
waiting for Charles Edward to look up.
Charles Edward has said nothing so far ;
you may have forgotten his existence.
Charles Edward has not had the heart
to speak since Dorinda appeared. He
makes a tragic figure as he stands in the
corner, gazing obstinately at his toes, and
turning two bright shillings over and over
in his pocket—shillings he has earned with
the earliest sweat of his brow and denied
himself cigarettes to keep intact, that he
may treat his little sweetheart to locusts
and honey-balls at St. Hender Feast. And
now, what awful miracle has been ac-
complished ? What tall unapproachable
divinity is this? This, the merry comrade
who so oft has shared his toffee, pocket-
warm, and paid him with a sticky kiss ?

Still Dorinda lingered, her magnetic
glance on the hapless youth, until at last

his eyes were irresistibly drawn to encounter hers. In his looks she read ample
confirmation of her mirror's story, and
she trilled a cruel laugh of triumph. It
was a dagger in his heart. Without a
word, without another look, he dashed
past her with lowered head, and flung
from the room, leaving the insolent beauty
to the enjoyment of her first triumph—
petty enough, perhaps, but giving earnest
of more glorious victories to come.

Still Dorinda lingered, dallying with
the moments, instinctively hesitating ere
she crossed the threshold and shut the
front door for ever on her childhood.
With her little hand hollowed out like a
rose-petal, she reflectively patted the shining coils of her hair ; a pretty gesture,
that comes untaught to new-born womanhood. She gazed about the room, and
discovered that it was full of mirrors ;

and at once her sobriety took wings. She danced like a butterfly round the walls, poising and peering at every polished surface; and everywhere—in the creampans and saucepans, in the picture-glasses, in the clock-cases — more or less shadowy and distorted Dorindas started forth to meet her. She caught up a big spoon from the table, and drew down her lips in mocking emulation of the grotesque tragedy-mask it presented to her view.

"Turn him t'other way about, my dear," said a voice behind her.

With a startled chirrup she spun and faced her father.

"Turn him about, my cheeld," Dickon repeated, "and he'll be laughing upon 'e, you'll find. And there you got the world in a gravy-spoon, merry or sad, according as you do take hold of 'm. But come— your ma 'll be wondering where we'm to.

40

Come ; you can take your old da's arm, if you ben't too proud."

" Dear daddy ! " she murmured, affectionately clinging to him. He glanced at her with admiring fondness.

" Old daddy's proud of his pretty daughter," he said. " And he an't a-going to read her no tejous old sarmons 'bout how she belong to behave now she's growed up. Some of these maids, now, they'm like bluebottles : honey or stale fish, 'tis all one to them, nor they can't taste of nother one without they get all of a mess. And a maid haven' got six legs, four to stand on while she clane herself with the other two. You take my maning, cheeld-vean ? "

" Yes, daddy, " she said, and squeezed his arm.

" That's right. Come along, then, and enjoy yourself. Plenty of honest fun in the world, thanks be. Come, my apple-blossom."

They had just stepped outside the door, when the sound of a throat a-clearing made them look up. At her bedroom window sat Mrs. Barron, a sallow, withered dame of sixty, with eyes like boot-buttons and a nose that had no secrets from her chin. The window being open, she was arrayed against the treacherous summer blasts in complete outdoor panoply — mushroom hat, heavily beaded cape, and gloves like hedgers' gauntlets. A pair of opera-glasses stood on the sill, convenient to her hand.

" Well, Emma," said Dickon, " how's your symptoms ? "

" Wisht, wisht," she replied, while her sharp eyes added Dorinda up from foot to head and back again. " Wisht, terrible wisht. Wake as a robin, sick as a shag.

42

You needn' be frightened to find a black-
face corp' hanging out o' window when
you come back-along."

"All right, Emma," he replied, cheer-
fully unappalled. "And how do 'e think
the maid's looking?"

"H'm! She won't feel lonely, I seem.
There's three gone up already the very
dapse of her—same hat, same dress, same
everything."

"But not the same face, I reckon,"
said Dickon, soothing away his daughter's
grimace of annoyance.

"There's fifty-seven people gone up
since twelve o'clock that I know by,"
continued Mrs. Barron. "Won't say but
there might be a few more crep' by
under the hedge. They're mean enough,
some of 'em. 'Tis your hedge, Dickon,
and if you were the good neighbour you
set yourself up to be, you'd trim it a deal

43

shorter, and cut down that gashly old apple-tree there to the gate. He've gone away up four feet since March month."

"How! Cut down Lord Derby! Why, Emma, there edn' a handsomer tree nor a more delicate bearer in all the orchard!"

"Handsome is as handsome does, and he get in the way something terrible after that. There might be a murder done to your very gate, and me setting here and not getting so much as a glimp' of it. But there! what do 'a matter? 'Twill soon be all one to me. If I live through the night, that's more 'n I've the right to expect. Who's that?"

The glasses were snatched up and brought to bear ; she bobbed to and fro, craning her neck, like an uneasy cormorant on a rock, and finally leaned sideways out of the window at an angle that

44

an active schoolboy would have considered risky.

"Only the Hamblys," she announced, recovering herself as briskly as Punch in the puppet-show. "Silas's rheumatics 'll be worse agin, by the way he walk. Sarah have got her reg'lar bottle of gin in her gown-pocket, I know, by the way she inched up to Silas so's to hide the bulge of it when she see me looking. Same old clo'es as last feast-day ; she've turned her cape, though, and a wisht poor job she've made of it. Fifty-nine. And not one of 'em got the dacency to step a yard aside and ask the state of my health. Mind, Dorinda, if anybody should inquire, I'm so bad as can be, and got three new symptoms since last week. That makes eleven, and if I knowed which one was going to carr' me off I'd die comfor'ble. But to go to your grave and never know

45

what's taking of 'e there—spasms or sciatic or inflammation or what—'tis enough to make 'e cut your throat."

" You'd be dead sure then, for sartain," commented Dickon. " Well, must be getting along, b'lieve."

" Hope you'll enjoy yourselfs, I'm sure," said Mrs. Barron lugubriously. " You needn't go worrying 'bout me, shut up all alone with nobody near in case of accident. If anything *should* happen, plaise-sure you won't know till you get back, so your holiday won't be spiled anyhow."

" Ouf ! " puffed Dickon under his breath as they moved away. " Emma's terrible malincholy to-day, poor soul. Must sarch out some tasty scandal to take back to her. You mind how bad she was last winter, till Mrs. Crapp down to cove took and run away with the fish-buyer. Cheered her up wonderful, that did ; she

46

was up and about for weeks after, so lively as a cricket. Ess, must see what we can do for her. But we won't cut down Lord Derby, will us, cheeld ? " he added as they approached that ancient worthy.

For answer, Dorinda took a step aside, put an arm about the tree, and patted its scarred trunk reassuringly with her soft hand. Such an action sits properly and prettily enough on a child or a young maiden ; but other folk had best think of their sins, and refrain from bestowing uninvited caresses on an aged and innocent creature who is powerless to respond or resist.

They found the others waiting for them at the foot of the hill. Here by the wayside—" tied to the hedge with a bremble," as the saying goes—stood the shop and. forge, shuttered and smokeless to-day, where Nicky and Hubert Barron plied

their trade. Here too the little river
sidled across the highway in a most friendly
and informal fashion, slipping unobserved
out of a gorse-thicket, spreading and sun-
ning itself in the road for a lazy silent
moment, and then gathering its robes
together for a dive under the footbridge,
and so away with a song among the
meadowsweet and ragged robin. I know
of no more delightful loitering-place than
this. There is the hill before you to
justify a halt; on working days there is
the smithy with its bright glow and merry
din—lives there a man so insensible to
the delights of colour and rhythm and
moving incident that he can resist the
invitation of a smithy door?—and there,
heedless of the clang of hammers, only
momentarily interrupted by passing traps
and waggons, a lively traffic of fish and
bird and beast goes on all day, along one

48

of Nature's own private thoroughfares.
Shoals of baby trout nuzzle at the water's
warm lip in the very middle of the road ;
white-masked wagtails rush to and fro
with twinkling legs, leaping suddenly into
the air, turning unexpectedly on their
heels as they run down their invisible
game ; a water-rat, that most ingenuous
and engaging of quadrupeds, goes leisurably across, half walking, half swimming
in the shallows, or sits combing his
whiskers on the bridge ; or a dowager
moorhen stalks past, bobbing her red top-
knot and shaking her white bustle, with
a crowd of youngsters tumbling after her,
each a fuzzy black ball touched with a
single scarlet point ; or a flash of brilliant
colour strikes across your eyes, and the
kingfisher is gone before you know he
has come. Right under the bridge a
water-ouzel sits with his white breast

against a stone, and chirps his hurried inarticulate water-song ; among the bushes on the other side of the way a sedge-warbler creaks and chides, and maliciously retails all the scandalous gossip of the hedgerows—what the frightened chaffinch said, and what the angry blackbird, and what the amorous thrush. There are rare secrets, no doubt, to be learned in dense forests and on trackless moors ; but some of us love best of all the easy familiarity of these wayside resting-places, where men and wild creatures go about their affairs without mutual hindrance, and Nature, like Sidney's Muse, "tempers her words to trampling horses' feet."

But Dorinda and her friends are already mounting the hill, and we must not linger behind. Note as you go how the road takes the ascent, with a mingling of caution and daring very characteristic of

the Cornish temperament ; starting cir-
cumspectly with a series of elaborate
curves and zigzags, and then, with the
stiffest bit of all before it, impatiently
throwing strategy to the winds, and storm-
ing the summit with a valiant charge.
There the grey tower of St. Hender
Church comes into sight, with sloping
blue roofs and rounded tree-tops heaped
about it. A gay flag floats on its summit ;
and out of its upper windows, like wild
bees from a rock, hurry endless flights of
swarming, humming notes that hang and
cluster, or speed anear, or flee and vanish
afar, in obedience to the gentle caprices
of the summer breeze. And now, with
your permission, we will step ahead of
our party, and set the scene for their
entrance on the Feast.

III

DISTINGUISHING St. Hender Churchtown in my memory from a score of other
tidy, clean, blue and grey upland villages,
I always begin by calling to mind the elm
trees that stand about the church. If you
are acquainted only with the hammer-
headed, warty-limbed monsters of the
midland hedge-rows, you will hardly recognize these slim beauties for their sisters.
No excrescences disfigure their shapely
stems, which shoot up, straight, lightly
plumed with twigs, and slender beyond
belief, to a height of forty feet or more,
before they fork and burst into a sheaf of
fine-leaved foliage. Their proportions are
scarcely stouter than those of a peacock's
feather, which they strikingly resemble in
profile. The least puff of air sets them

rocking; in a gale they bend and toss like young dancing Mænads. There is something so exquisitely feminine in the appearance of these airy, flexile creatures, that a man is bound to lose his heart to them at sight. You may remember that the two most lovable young women in all the world of books—Nausicäa and Clara Middleton—are compared by their creators to trees: the one to a young palm tree, and the other to a silver birch in a breeze. When first I described Dorinda with a profusion of images drawn from Nature's store-house, I likened her, not inappropriately, to a young poplar; but if I may now be permitted to withdraw the poplar, and substitute one of her own native elms, I shall feel happy in the modest assurance that my heroine will hold her own with Homer's and Mr. Meredith's, at least so far as the comparison will carry her.

53

Excepting the elms, St. Hender has little to distinguish it from its neighbours. It consists mainly of a double row of houses up street, with doorsteps giving on the road, and a scattering of other houses down street, standing back behind gardens. The down-street folk are doubtful of the gentility of the up-street folk ; the up-street folk have no doubts at all about the morality of the down-street folk. The church, a chapel, a school, a shop, and a policeman serve the material and moral needs of all.

The revels are not yet at their height, but a numerous company is already assembled. Some parade the street, where the chief attraction is a row of " standings" or stalls for the sale of sweetmeats. Many have already found their way into the glebe meadow, where races are being run, and the Harmonious Rechabites—Wesleyans and teetotalers all—are pounding and groping their brazen and indomitable way through the variegated layers—quick slow, loud, soft, martial, pathetic—of a Sacred Fantasia. A select assembly is mustered in the churchyard, where they stand in silent groups with bowed heads, like moorland cattle in a storm, under the pelting rain of sounds that gushes from the belfry. Here is the Vicar in the midst of a little group of quality-folk, who are doing their best to enjoy them-, selves immensely. If now and then a delicate hand goes up to a ladylike ear you perceive in a moment that it is only to pat a stray lock into place. Yonder with watches and note-books are the judges : two farmers, a curate, a retired butcher—it is a noteworthy, and to house-holders a suspicious, fact that the world is full of retired butchers, many of them in

the prime of life—and the chief engineer
to the local district council : he, I mean,
who steers the steam-roller with such
skill and judgment over the hills and
dales of fifteen crumpled parishes. Art
knows no social grades ; their heads are
in confidential proximity, and one and
all wear an identical expression on
their faces—an expression hard to de-
scribe, but to be seen any day at flower-
shows and other places where judicial func-
tions are imposed on the amateur. It is
intended, I believe, to indicate a subtle
combination of thoughtful attention, strict
impartiality, and modest deprecation of
greatness neither born to nor achieved.

Here and there you will observe ancient
men seated on flat tombstones with stubs
of pencils in their hands. From time to
time the pencils go up to their mouths ;
a moment of deliberation, and a hiero-

glyph is inscribed on the sepulchral slate. These are the unofficial critics—campano- logical enthusiasts, who have an intimate acquaintance with all the peals for miles around and can tell you the weight, tonal qualities, and private idiosyncrasies of every constituent bell. Presently it will be their painful duty to condemn and re- fute the judges' awards, and one another's decisions as well. Long after the rest of the company has departed, the tide of argument will continue to surge about those peaceful headstones.

'Now your attention is directed to several groups of six men each, who stand apart, talking but little, and that in undertones, shadowed by the near approach of a great responsibility. Of one group you take particular notice. Five are old- sters, the sixth is in the prime of well-set- up young manhood. On Hubert Barron, the neophyte, the shadow is deepest. He wipes a moist hand on a coat-flap, he jigs a nervous knee, he bores holes in the turf with his stick ; he wishes his father hadn't been so ready to thrust him forward ; he wishes he had followed his youthful impulse ten years ago and run away to sea ; he wishes he were under the grass in that cool unoccupied corner down there by the sycamore. In short, Hubert has a bad attack of stage-fright. His father —that tall, gaunt old man with the goat-beard—has anxiously noted it, and is wisely refraining from any attempt to dispel it, while thanking his stars that the turn of the home team comes next.

The clamour in the belfry quickened, doubled, slowed again, as bell after bell was brought down, and suddenly ceased, leaving a confused hum of overtones and undertones in every ear. The tombstone critics totted up their marks ; the judges scribbled in their note-books, exchanged a few pregnant words and nods, and relaxed their facial identity to a variety of every-day expressions. The Vicar detached him-self from his guests and hurried across to the St. Hender champions.

" Now, friends," he said in his hyper-bolically genial week-a-day manner, which was so disconcertingly unlike his profes-sional pulpit manner, and bore no resem-blance at all to his natural manner, which last was known only to his wife and possibly his bishop : " Now, friends, your turn next. Keep steady, thirty rounds to the minute, and don't forget you've the credit of our dear old parish in your hands."

" That's all right, Mr. Trevelyan. Trust us else."

" A pretty ' touch,' that last," continued

the Vicar, airing his acquaintance with belfry technicalities. "But I think we can show them a better—aha, Barron?"

"'Tis to be hoped we do," replied Nicky. "Pretty ringing, as you do say; so nate and clane as ever I heard from an up-the-country team. But we'm at home, that's where 'tis,—with our own bells, that we do know without book from rope-end to clapper so well as we do know our own wives, and better p'r'aps. So don't you fret, Mr. Trevelyan. Barring accidents, we'm safe enough, I reckon."

"That's right, that's right. Now, here come the others. In with you, and good luck."

The two teams passed each other, exchanging looks carefully stripped of all expression, rivalry and fellow-artistry cancelling one another and leaving a cipher for a result. At the belfry door stood

60

William Bone the sexton, keeping guard. St. Hender's ringing chamber was small and cramped, and the autocratic Nicky set his face sternly against the admission of idle spectators, even at practices ; much more on such a critical occasion as this.

"Now mind, Billy," said he. "Door shut home so soon as we'm inside, and no admission, not if 'tis the Vicar himself."

"Not if 'twas the Pope of Rome, with a bundle of firewood under aich arm, and 'Leave me geek or you burn' 'pon his lips!" was the emphatic answer.

They filed in, and the door closed upon them. In silence they hung up their hats and coats, took each man his allotted place, and coiled each man the loose end of his rope in readiness. Nicky cast a rapid glance overhead, down along the ropes, at the floor, at the door, and lastly at his men, dwelling for a moment on

Hubert, and noting with satisfaction that all signs of nervousness had vanished.

" Ready ! "

They grasped the fellets, or handling-tufts, which are more commonly known as " sallies "—I suppose on account of their resemblance to the fluffy catkins of the goat-willow or sallow.

" Go ! "

With military precision they turned sideways, so that each member of the circle had his eye on the rope of the bell he was to follow in the opening rounds.

" Gone ! "

Each man in turn, from treble to tenor, bore gently and firmly on his rope. There followed that moment of dignified silence which so surprises and impresses the uninitiated spectator, used as he is to the pertly instantaneous response of the vulgar house-bell ; and then, muffled, sweet, even, nicely graded as a string of pearls, the answering voices of the imprisoned monsters swam out on high. Nothing gives more delight to the understanding eye and ear than this quaint little ritual of the rising of the bells. And to think that in some benighted parishes they are risen separately in a distressing sequence of solitary jangles, as if a drunken man or mischievous child were tugging at the ropes haphazard !

Precisely at that moment our friends from Sunny Corner arrived at the crying-cross by the churchyard gate. There they separated : Mr. Varco to flit from group to group, showering quips as he went; Mrs. Varco to enter the first of the hospitably open doors behind which it was her intention to spend the rest of the day in a series of comfortable chats with

old cronies ; Miss Roscorla to search for
Charles Edward, unaccountably vanished
and held under suspicion of clandestine
cigarette-smoking ; Mr. Roscorla into
the churchyard, there to sit and confer
with his stick on a convenient tombstone ;
and Dorinda to join for the first time the
band of grown-up maidens, who paraded
the street, arm in arm, a fresh and fra-
grant nosegay of beauties.   Her we follow
as in duty bound.

She was greeted with critical stares and
scornful giggles, and a voice that said—

"Go away, little girl, and play with
the little boys."

But Dorinda, with a laugh and a jest,
took the speaker irresistibly by the waist,
and joined in the light chatter that I dare
not pen on paper, lest I soil its butterfly
wings.   In two minutes, by sheer force
of personality, she was the acknowledged

leader of the band ; and when the question arose, where to go and what to do next, it was she who carried the day with her suggestion that the folk in the church-yard looked terrible solid and mopish, and why not go and cheer them up a bit ?

In they poured through the lych-gate, and swept round the church, lifting their voices three parts in laughter and one part in talk. Young men, perched here and there on the churchyard wall, cast longing glances on them as they passed, but none was found so bold as to engage the raillery of a dozen maidenly tongues at once. With light feet they trampled the dust of generations, and once and again they gathered about a headstone, and a young voice put warmth and music into a cold *hic jacet*.

At his post by the belfry door, Mr. Bone regarded them with a disapproving eye ; and at last, as for the third time they fluttered twittering past him, he raised his voice in hoarse reprobation.

"Shame upon 'e, maidens, chattering and laughing among the silent tombs !"

The bevy paused and wheeled like a flock of linnets.

"'Tis Billy Bone, the crotchety old toad. Under the harrow with him !"

"Who steals the church candle-ends and takes them home to start the fire with ?"

"Billy Bone !"

"Who went to sleep one Sunday and said Amen in the middle of the discourse ?"

"Billy Bone !"

"Who starved his wife for the sake of her burying fee ?" I regret to say that Dorinda was responsible for this scandalous insinuation.

"Billy Bone ! Oh, Billy Bone !"

Mr. Bone's wrath overflowed into shout-
ings.

"Ah, ye flirtingills ! Ah, ye daughters
of Babylon ! In white and blue and pink
I behold 'e, but scarlet's your proper wear.
Keep back from the door there, will 'e ? "

" Who's keeping the snuggest corner of
all for his own trumpery old carcase ? "

" Billy Bone. Shame upon 'e, Billy
Bone ! "

Duty was forgot. " Out of the churchyard with 'e ! " shouted Billy, advancing
with waving arms upon the flock, which
scattered with shrill cries before him.
Who was it that doubled back, and all
unseen darted to the door and turned the
prohibited handle ? Who but Dorinda,
her normal feminine curiosity stimulated
by a desire to prove and confirm her
new-found womanhood with a taste of
forbidden fruit ?

F 2   67

DORINDA'S BIRTHDAY

Cautiously she pushed open the door a few inches and peeped within.

A shaft of sunlight slanted from an upper window into her eyes. Dimly seen in the dusty sonorous gloom beyond, six silent figures lifted their arms to heaven and bowed themselves, as if they were engaged in some strange devotional ceremony. It was a sight that few of her sex have been privileged to set eyes on, and to her irreverent and uncomprehending eyes I fear it was a foolishly comical sight ; had she dared, she would have laughed aloud at the ridiculous figures these rapt artists cut at their unintelligible game. No two of them tackled their ropes in the same fashion. Wizened old Michael Cock at the tenor bell squatted at every down-stroke like the bottom man in a sawpit, his knees flying abroad after the manner of a swimming frog's. At the fourth bell, Mason Tripcony doubled himself up like a two-foot rule, grunting softly as one vexed with an inward pain. At the third, Bartle the shoemaker ducked with a sudden jerk, avoiding some invisible missile ; Roger Tregear at the second swept a polite but distant bow to a ghostly acquaintance. Nicky Barron, the treble, was the skilfullest ringer with the lightest bell. Of him it had been admiringly said that, once his bell was risen, he could ring it with a needleful of thread. Except for his hands and arms he scarcely moved at all, but remained stiffly upright, rocking almost imperceptibly from the hips upwards, a precise piece of machinery rather than a man. The ringer of the fifth bell was the only one of the set who could be called graceful. Lithe, upstanding, effortless, not so much clutching the

fellet at each return as allowing it to slip
into his hand, swaying slightly and easily,
bowing ever so little, Hubert might have
been the one human figure in a group of
grotesque automata. He was ringing his
best, and tasting the joys of skilled and
numbered exercise as only the expert
ringer can. The rope was a part of
himself—a long, flexible feeler communi-
cating between his brain and the spot,
overhead and out of sight, where his
great bell poised itself mouth upwards on
the balance, or swept free through its
circular journey, sensitively respondent
at each pause to his firm yet delicate
control. The little enclosed chamber was
a world apart—a world of ordered rhythm,
sequestered from the confused and tumultuous world of men by thick walls of
impenetrable granite. Rhythmically he
and his companions bent and swung ;

rhythmically the ropes tap-tapped on the floor and rustled between their hands ; rhythmically they rattled through the fellet-holes above ; and rhythmically from on high came the soothed music of the dancing bells. At other times Hubert was no more noteworthy for comeliness of feature or grace of gesture than the first young rustic you might meet in the lanes ; but now, giving and taking motion in music, with parted lips and eyes that seemed intent on some celestial vision, he was transfigured out of his ordinary self. And it was at this fortunate moment, carefully selected by Destiny, that Dorinda first saw him with her new-washed womanly eyes. She saw, and wonderingly admired. Here was the Hubert of every day and all the year round, the big boy neighbour who was as familiar, and about as emotionally impressive as the

71

water-butt, or Lord Derby, or the family mangle, suddenly transmuted into something new and strange. It was a terrible funny feeling, she allowed. And he was certainly a proper young fellow.

Some three seconds had now elapsed since Dorinda first peeped in at the door. If to the reader the time has seemed considerably longer, that is not altogether the writer's fault. The stuff he works in is at least partly to blame, compelling him as it does to cram the three dimensions into one, and to express everything, fixed or transitory, solid, plane, or altogether unbounded, in terms of an ever-moving line of words. Some day, perhaps, there will arise among story-tellers an innovator bold enough to dispose of all his comments, incidental descriptions, and lengthy analyses of momentary emotions, by packing them away in small

72

print at the foot of the page, where they will not obstruct the flow of the narrative, and may be skipped at pleasure by the large and respectable class that cares nothing for these things.

Three seconds, then, had elapsed, when the leader broke silence with an order—

" Fifth to third."

They were ringing in the old-fashioned, easy-going, rustic way—so sneered at by the self-styled scientific ringers, but not to be despised for that reason—in which each change in the sequence of the bells, instead of being immediately abandoned in favour of another, was repeated a sufficient number of times for all the world to get comfortably accustomed to it. At this moment they were nearing the end of the touch (like the Vicar, I know enough to refrain from calling it a peal), known to west-country ringers as " The

Queen's Sixties." The treble bell was
"hunting," or threading its way among
the other bells, from the first place to the
fifth and back again. Each time it reached
the end of its journey in either direction,
it waited its turn, while two of the other
bells made what is called a cross change.
It was one of these cross changes that was
now called by Nicky; the import of it
being that Hubert was to "hold-up" or
check his bell in the next round, so as to
allow the third bell to cut in before him.
To do this, he had to turn about a little,
so as to get his eye on the rope of his
new leader. Doing this he would also
face the door.

Hubert turned, and at the same moment
Dorinda, her curiosity freshly stimulated
by Nicky's announcement, pushed the door
open an inch or two further. Hubert
allowed his attention to wander for an

instant from the critical business in hand, and was lost—his wits scattered to the winds before a vision of smiling beauty set in a glory of sunshine. In a moment he recovered himself, but just by the length of that moment he had checked his bell too long, and immediately Five and Two clanged together in horrid discord. The vision promptly vanished, like a pantomime fairy when the demon strikes the gong.

"Stiddy, stiddy!" exclaimed Nicky with anxious vehemence. But Hubert's nerves refused to be steadied. The shadow of disgrace was on him, and through the shadow danced a vivid bewildering phantom of sunlit loveliness. He blundered desperately on, colliding violently with his neighbours on either side, rudely jostling the treble as it attempted to slip past him on its way home, and finally committing the unpardonable sin of losing his place altogether. A course of bells is an intricate dance in an extremely circumscribed area; if one performer falls out of step, the whole figure is thrown into confusion. The orderly circle of sounds began to crumble; ugly gaps, disgraceful dotted notes, marred its symmetry in every direction. The bells themselves in their high prison became aware of the want of unanimity among their masters, and began at once to take sly liberties; for a church bell—as everyone who has handled rope in belfry has good reason to know—is not a mere mass of inanimate metal, but a more or less christianized servant of the Church, with a dim soul and a very decided will of its own. The hands of the Church have been laid on it in benediction; nay, in some cases it has actually been baptized with all the proper ceremonies; and something of the old Adam, turbulent and unruly, has somehow slipped into it in the process. Under firm control it is a willing and obedient servant; but let discipline be relaxed ever so little, and there is no end to the impish, choir-boy tricks it will play.

Luckily the course was nearly run. Cool and unruffled, picking out the least disorderly moments in which to call the few remaining changes, Nicky shepherded his flock back into the straight, steadied them there, and gave the signal " Down " for the final quickening.

Scarcely had he given the terminal stamp of the foot, when four disappointed and disgraced old men turned looks of bitter reproach on Hubert, who stood with bowed head awaiting the storm.

But Nicky spoke before it could burst.

"Not a word, comrades, not a word! The fault's on two, and neither one's my son. You all know me—a just man that put the fault where it belong, whether 'tis my own flesh and blood or no. The fault's on two; one we do know, and t'other shall be sarched out before the sun do set upon this day of sorrow. Say what you've a mind to say to Billy Bone; he deserve whatever he get. But as for the maid, you leave her to me."

"Maid, sayst?" piped the tenor bell.

"Yes, Michael. Yes, fellow-ringers. A maid, sure enough. Didn' I glimp' her geeking in to the door? Out of the corner of my eye I glimped her, with her outrageous fallals and fancicals, 'nough to put any young man's bell off his balance."

"Maid in the belfry? Who ever heard

78

tell of such a thing? Stark agin nature,
so 'tis."

"Don't know about that, Michael,"
said Mason Tripcony. "Take a twice-
married man's word for 'n, the females do
nat'rally belong to be azackly where they
don't belong to be. Well, we've lost first
prize, that's certain."

"Lost first prize!" quoth Roger
Tregear. "'Twill be more'n we deserve
if we 'm highly condemned, as the man
said. Who was the maid, Nicky?"

"That's what I'm going to sarch out,
if I do live. 'A was too quick for me, the
artful piece, but I should know her agin
by the colour of her dress, I reckon."

"But Hubert here see her plain enough,
didn' 'a?"

All eyes were turned on Hubert, who
flushed and paled under his tan. It
appeared from his evidence, oozing out

drop by drop under paternal pressure, that he never noticed the maid, if maid she was, at all ; that if he did, there was no time to make her out properly ; that he was sure, by what he did see of her, that she was a stranger to him ; that he didn't remark what she had on ; that he rather thought she was dressed in pink trimmed up with white, and not the other way about ; and that anyhow the fault rested entirely with him, and what did it matter who the maid was ?

Nicky frowned suspiciously at this lucid statement.

" Tell 'e what, comrades," he said darkly. " There's something behind all this. You know me ; I can smell out a roguery in the dark so well as most; and if there an't no roguery here, I'll eat my bell-rope. A cooked job, sure 'nough, and I'm going to sarch en out. Ayther 'tis somebody got a gredge agin us, or else——" He broke off, with another suspicious glance at his son. "But leave en to me ; and mind 'e—not a word of this outside. Must catch 'em off their guard, whoever they be."

"There's bitter moments waiting for us outside," prophesied Michael. "Mr. Trevelyan—can't 'e hear en, with his 'Tut-tut, friends !' and his 'Honour of our dear old parish' ? Aw, bitter !"

"We got to face en," said Nicky, as they huddled on their coats. "Best face en like men, shoulder to shoulder, stand or fall together, faithful comrades one and all. Come along, boys."

Hubert was the last to go out. Looking back, Nicky saw him before the little looking-glass that hung by the door, carefully settling his necktie, anxiously fingering his chin. Nicky nodded grimly.

IV

In the formula with which the old
romancer loosely but sufficiently hooks
chapter on to rambling chapter, now leave
we of the ringers and turn we unto the
damosel Dorinda, as she slips away unobserved from the fatal door, all unconscious of the havoc she has wrought.

Like Spenser's bride, she went on with
portly pace, and eyes affixèd on the lowly
ground, her thoughts for once in a way
turned inwards and pensively examining a
new-born fancy—emotion I can hardly
call it as yet—that waved vague hands and
fluttered filmy wings somewhere down in
a corner of her bosom. It seemed—but I
shrink from pouncing on this half-uncon-
scious baby Cupid and ruthlessly dissect-

ing its tender limbs for the delectation of the gloating multitude. Besides, the most skilful anatomist of the female heart would find his knife too blunt and his fingers too clumsy for the job.

When again she lifted her head, she found herself walking among long grass on the deserted north side of the church. A little farther on, Mr. Roscorla sat solitary on his chosen tombstone. For the better easing of his thought-laden brow, he had removed his hat and had hung it on the knobby head of his walking-stick, which leaned against the stone beside him and appeared to be whispering dark secrets in his attentive ear. He saw Dorinda approaching, and straightway set a match to a welcoming smile, which, kindling by degrees, reached its full effulgence as she paused in front of him. She smiled back, and appeared to expect a remark. Well,

he had one ready on his tongue—a tried
and approved remark.

" Fine growing weather for the craps,"
said he, and smiled and smiled, confidently
expectant of the prescribed and tested
retort. But Dorinda only set a merry
laugh running up the wild bird's gamut,
and so tripped away and left him without a word. He gazed after her, inwardly
puzzled, and disappointed not a little,
though his outward expression was un-
changed. A smile like that, built up (to
vary my similitude) with such laborious
care, is not to be hurriedly demolished in
a moment, like a triumphal arch as soon
as the royal guest has passed through. It
remained fixed while he watched her out
of sight. Even then it stood a while forgotten, what time he obscurely ruminated
on the incalculable feminine, until the
stretched and stiffened muscles signalled

for relief, and garland by garland, timber by timber, the festal structure was demolished, and the ploughed field resumed its normal aspect.

Dorinda stood once more in the street, uncertain of her direction. But what did it matter? Wherever she went, she was sure of admiring glances and approving smiles, and (best of all) envious, would-be scornful sniffs. It was her seventeenth birthday, and the feast was being held in her honour, and the sun had engaged himself to stay up to the latest possible moment, expressly for her sake.

As she danced down the street, she fancied she heard her mother's voice within an open doorway. She drew near and looked, and there, sure enough, was Mrs. Varco enjoying the hospitality of Mrs. Pedrick's kitchen.

If Mrs. Varco was large, Mrs. Pedrick

was enormous—a mere chaos of intersecting globes ; her eyes and nose and mouth were little round sofa-buttons in the luxurious crimson upholstery of her cheeks, her apron-strings an equatorial line about a purely theoretical waist. But while Mrs. Varco's easy soul lolled comfortably among its fleshly cushions, Mrs. Pedrick's active spirit bustled about its monstrous tabernacle, a bumble-bee in a many-domed conservatory. Side by side they sat, these jolly dames, and rolled together, exchanging confidences, and rolled apart, quivering and bobbing, for all the world like two toy balloons on one string.

"And who may this fitty maid be ?" inquired Mrs. Pedrick good-humouredly.

"Why, 'tis Dorinda! Step inside, cheeld, and taste of Mis' Pedrick's saffern cake."

" Ess, step inside, my dear. No charge
to see the fat woman. Take a chair and
a slice, then, while I look 'e over. Ess, a
fitty maid, and do your ma credit. She
was just such another, five-and-twenty
year ago ; so was I, though you mightn'
think it. And here I sit for slender maids
to take warning by, a reg'lar old skelinton
at the feast—ho-ho ! But I an't complain-
ing. Keeps us out of a lot o' mischief,
don't 'a, Tamsine ? To think of the
pranks we might be up to, and our
husbands out of sight, if only we wadn'
afraid of melting away like tallow-candles
in the sun, and back come our men, and
' Where's my woman ? ' and ' Where's
mine ? '—and the neighbours a-p'inting
mournful to two cages of bones in a
puddle of grease, middle of the road—ho-
ho ! "

If Dorinda's polite laughter was a little

forced, who can blame her? A vulgar old woman, to be sure; and what a tedious subject to make a jest of! Given a preposterously stout parent, even slender seventeen cannot refrain from uneasy speculations on the problem of heredity.

"Seeming to me, though," said Mrs. Varco, "you do get about a brave lot more than what I do, Mary. Mis' Pedrick have just come home from London, Dorinda — been to see the sights."

"See the sights!—yes, and a wisht job I had seeing of 'em too, I can tell 'e. Wherever they took me, 'twas the same— Waxworks, Tower of London, Crystal Palace, I stuck in the turnstile every time, and no getting of me for'ard or back'ard. And Pedrick a-shoving, and the p'liceman a-hauling, and the people standing round laughing and cheering—la! what fun we did have, to be sure ! Sights ! I was the principal sight myself, b'lieve ! "

Dorinda smiled constrainedly, and fidgeted on her seat. A most indelicate circumstance, with nothing funny about it that she could see. Mrs. Pedrick's sharp, good-natured eyes noted the signs of impatience.

" Finished up your cake, my dear ? Dagging to be off, shouldn't be frightened. Off with 'e then, fitty maid, so soon 's you've a mind to. Didn' come up to do the polite to fat old women, did 'e ?' Found a chap yet ? "

" Maybe I have, maybe I haven't," said Dorinda, more pertly, I am constrained to admit, than befits a heroine.

" Well, no time like feast-time for that. Maids' harvest, I call en. I catched mine 'pon a feast-day, and so did your ma here. Same day too ; wadn' 'a, Tamsine ? Do 'e

mind how I took up with Dickon first
go-off, and you with Pedrick, till we got
to the stile-path going home, and then
we chopped by way of a joke, you taking
my chap and me taking yourn ? 'Twadn'
much of a joke to begin with, b'lieve, but
la ! how it have lasted ! Hey, Tamsine ? "

Chuckling hugely, they fell on each
other with ponderous slaps and digs.
Dorinda curled her lip and moved to the
door.

" Dickon didn' like it at all to begin
with," said Mrs. Varco.

" Same for Pedrick. No mouth-speech,
and glimping behind every minute to see
what you 'uns were up to.   But 'a squeezed
my waist out of politeness, like, getting
over the first stile, and then I managed
him so well that I got en to kiss me agin
my will, top of the second.   And there
'tis.   You spin 'pon your heel for light-

someness, or you geek through a door for mischief, and—'There's your life-road,' says Providence, and no turning round for ever afterwards. So mind how you step, my dear."

Dorinda tittered nervously. Who or what had inspired this voluble fat old thing to speak in the same breath of doors and destinies? She scorned to be superstitious, but when blindfolded Chance hammers a little out-of-the-way nail plumb on the head, it is a token not to be despised.

"But la! Tamsine," continued Mrs. Pedrick. "If only our men could ha' seen us then like what we are now! Old Providence 'ud ha' been properly took in, I reckon! Now there's my daughter Ellen; she know her way about, b'lieve. Catched her man somewhere up the country—never brought en down to be introduced, nor never let en set eyes 'pon

me, not till the banns were up, and no
chance for a hon'rable chap to back out.
But 'a took it very well when 'a did see
me, I will say that for him ; so quiet as a
lamb 'a took it, and never turned a hair,
though I couldn' help rallying of him
a bit.

"'There an't no bounds to my affection
for Ellen,' 'a said to me, in a voice like
milk-and-water with a drop of gin into it.
So I said : 'Just as well,' I said ; 'if she's
going to turn after her ma you'll want
some elbow-room later on,' I said. So
he said : 'As the years do pass, so my
love shall grow,' 'a said. 'Shouldn' be
frightened if she did,' I said. 'Hold
tongue, mother,' says Ellen. 'I didn'
name it that way,' he said ; 'though if so
be I did, what's a few score extry pounds
to a love like mine ? Can't have too
much of a good thing, b'lieve,' says he,

92

goggling 'pon Ellen, fond-like. 'Silly fool!' says Ellen, looking like she wanted to stick a knife into both of us. But la! —must have my joke, b'lieve, or I'd be wasting away, as Aunt Maria said for the soap, Monday arternoon. Laugh and grow fat—hey, Tamsine?''

Again they wallowed together, exchanging thumps and nudges, while Dorinda, properly disgusted, slipped away without a formal farewell.

Whither now? What had become of her late companions? Here came one of them—Laura Pengelly, sure enough, with Harry Laity in tow. *She* hadn't been wasting her time, seemingly.

As they approached, Harry stared hard at Dorinda, and whispered to Laura, who answered with a short word and a tost head. Harry still stared, and seemed inclined to slacken pace. Laura clutched his elbow

93

and hustled him by, with a distant patronizing nod to Dorinda in passing. And a quarter of an hour ago they were twining arms and waists, and on the point of swearing eternal friendship ! A hollow world, to be sure ! As if she were likely to grudge a fellow like Harry to a girl like Laura ! As soon would she take up with poor half-baked Jack there, tacking up the street with his ragged coat-tails flying and the lining of his battered pilot-cap hanging jauntily out on one side for bravery. It wasn't everybody, either, that Jack would favour with his company and conversation. Jack was noted as a discriminating admirer of the sex, with as keen an eye for a pretty face as any one. To number him among one's cavaliers was a positive distinction.

"Oh, Jack !" she called sweetly.

Jack stopped, dodged, and began to

94

sidle round by the gutter. Politeness showed a gap-toothed grin, but suspicion clouded his little wandering eyes.

"Nicely thank'ee hope all well home fine day *good* arternoon," he remarked with telegraphic conciseness and despatch, and dodged to the other side of the road.

"Where going in such a hurry, Jack?" she cooed, squandering one of her best smiles as she followed him. "Can't 'e stop and chat with a poor lonely maid? What's that you got in your hand there? Something for me, I'll be bound."

Jack whipped his clenched fist behind him. "Leave me pass, and I'll tell 'e," he growled, and made a sudden ungainly rush which brought him safely beyond her. "What I got in my hand?" he cackled triumphantly over his shoulder as he ambled away. "Got a ha'penny in my hand! Where going? Going to put en

95

away safe before one o' these poor lonely maids do get hold o' me ! "

" Had 'e there," said a voice at Dorinda's elbow. She whirled about, and found herself in the presence of four old men, who stood in a row across the road, leaning on their sticks and gravely contemplating her, like so many owls on a rafter.

" Had 'e there, b'lieve," repeated the spokesman. "There's some do call Jack a fool, but he know a thing or two after that, if you'll believe a twice-married man, who've tried buttons to his pockets, and stockings up the chimley, and savings-banks, and look to die fourpence in debt after all. Ess, there's bigger fools than Jack going around with money in their fistes. Try agin, my dear, and better luck next time."

Insufferable old man ! If a glance could kill, he would never pull bell-rope again.

96

With skirts drawn away from degrading contact, she swept through the line. It closed up behind her, and four sets of grey whiskers wagged in a whispered colloquy.

" White trimmed up with pink ! That's the maid—that's of her ! "

" Where's Nicky to ?   Must leave him know to once."

" Varco's maid, edn' 'a ?   A dashy, impident piece, by the looks of her ; know all the roguery there is, I'll be bound."

" Keep an eye 'pon her, some of 'e. I'll go see for Nicky."

But Dorinda, her feet winged with indignation, was already out of sight. When the devoted chronicler and (I hope) not unreluctant reader catch her up, she is entering the glebe meadow, where the band is now doing remorseless execution on a *pot-pourri* of hymn tunes, while at the farther end the sports committee marshals the competitors in a blindfold wheelbarrow race. There is a tidy sprinkling of folk about, but the meadow is of large extent, and when once Dorinda has slipped through the crowd by the gate she is able to indulge her present desire for solitude. As she wanders lonely by the hedge, I mark the pout of her lips and the moody bent of her brow; and anxiously, but hopefully, I note that a divine discontent is working within her. The finer fibres of her nature are awake and stirring; small wonder if she finds herself temporarily at odds with this gross world of obese old women, and cynical old men, and suspicious fools, and faithless friends. It is only temporarily, I promise you. Elastic youth soon readjusts itself to its environment.

Suddenly a warning shout was raised, and down the field, at first in parallel lines, but soon diverging, concurring, crossing, colliding, like fortuitous atoms of a world in the making, rushed the blindfold barrow-trundlers with their helpless human burdens. Women shrieked and brave men fled, while the sports committee ran to and fro, waving ineffectual arms and shouting futile injunctions, like bungling magicians who had rashly decanted a whole binful of bottled genii. The band, threatened by an earnest and bulky competitor with a particularly massive barrow, faltered, broke off, and scattered in all directions. So the peaceful and melodious denizens of the African forest scatter before the mad onrush of a hunted elephant; and as the frantic pachyderm crashes through a copse of young trees, and leaves behind him a pathway strewn with splintered and uprooted saplings, even so driver, vehicle, and wild-bellowing passenger plunged among the spindly music-stands, brought them clattering to the ground, and pounded on, unscathed and unheeding.

Dorinda, observing the scene with a tristful smile, was suddenly aware of another blind emissary of fate tilting straight towards her. With a shriek she dodged, taking shelter behind a wild-rose thicket, and so came upon Charles Edward.

Pale, pensive, embowered in roses, Charles Edward reclined on the velvet sward, the pattern of a love-sick shepherd swain in a pastoral. Beside him on the turf, where crook and flageolet should have been, lay a paper bag half full of pear-drops, a box of matches, a new briar pipe, and a packet of Old Salt mixture—not the mild effeminate quality in the green wrapper, but the full and nutty brand with the orange label. Disillusioned, heart-sore, world-weary, Charles Edward had been seeking oblivion in reckless dissipation, and had learned already that when you take your passions to market, woe for woe is the only barter.

On Dorinda's appearance he sat up, took his pipe, lit a match, thrust a momentary weakness from him, and resolutely sucked the flame in, watching Dorinda out of the corner of his eye. Dorinda said nothing, but stood regarding him with a faint smile, which might mean anything else, but certainly did not mean admiration. Yet it is fabled that the quality of qualities to attract a woman in a man is manliness. Charles Edward ground his teeth into the vulcanite, and puffed on. The damp tobacco, inexpertly kindled, burned with a subterranean fire, spitting and sparkling like saltpetre, and tasting nearly as nasty. Charles Edward doggedly puffed on.

Dorinda noted his increasing pallor with mingled pity and alarm. She wrinkled her pretty nose, and remarked to the roses that no gentleman would think of smoking in a lady's presence without permission asked and accorded. Outwardly impassive, inwardly grateful, he risked one more puff out of bravado, and set the pipe down. Dorinda sank gracefully beside him.

" Well ? " she said.

Charles Edward grunted. At that moment he did not wish to open his mouth in speech.

" Ben't you going to offer me one little sweetie ? "

He pushed the bag towards her. She helped herself and held it out for him to do the same. He waved it away with a shudder.

" You can have the lot," he mumbled, cautiously sliding the words out. She thanked him sweetly, and sat thoughtfully munching. Her brief experience of womanhood had not been deliriously satisfying. It was good to be a child again for a while, with her childhood's companion by her side to coax or tease at pleasure.

Charles Edward, feeling a little better, glanced round, caught her smiling eye, and made answer with a sheepish grin. They began to talk confidentially as of yore.

" Where been all this time, Charlie ? "

" Aw, diddling around, 'a b'lieve."

" You were in a terrible hurry to be off, I seem. Might have waited for your old chum, I think."

" Might so well have stayed home altogether," he replied morosely. " Tell 'e what 'tis—Hender Feast an't what it's cracked up to be. It's gone in considerable since I was a little tagger."

Dorinda agreed with a sigh. A fellow-feeling brought her cuddling closer to her companion. His spirits rose. He ran a carelessly ostentatious finger round between his collar and his neck, and ventured on a regular grown-up compliment.

"How nice your hair do look, Dorinda!"

She laughed contentedly. If Charles Edward could talk like that, he deserved encouragement.

"Shall I tell 'e a secret, Charlie? I've got thirty-five hairpins into 'n, and I do feel so awful complicated up top. Can't see some sticking out, can 'e?"

The back of her head was offered to his inspection. There was a minikin ear lodged in a coil of hair—a delicate rosy shell in a lock of gleaming brown sea-weed. The creamy nuddick—nape you would call it—sun-visited for the first

time to-day, was set about with darling
tendrils, curled trammels, feathery lures,
pisky springes to entangle hearts in.
Above, a great shining wave billowed out
and curved back into the shadow of the
hat. Some women's heads of hair are
no better than mere inanimate wigs;
some have the dim imperfect vitality of
plants; but some—and Dorinda's was of
these—thrill with life to the tips of every
strand. They are electric, serpentine,
mysterious, and exhale that subtle odour
of the sea which clings for ever to the
tresses of the sea-born goddess.

Charles Edward wove no fancies half
so fine as these, which have mainly been
conveyed from the poets. Deep emotions
do not dally with elegant conceits, and
Charles Edward's emotions were positively
abysmal.

"There's one 'll be dropping out directly,

if you don't push him in," he said hoarsely.

"Push him in for me, will 'e?" said she, inclining towards him with a sweet abandonment.

He advanced a trembling finger and did the sacred office. Who would have thought that the mere touch of those gossamer tresses could so thrill and sting? His smouldering passion burst into sudden flame.

"Aw, Dorinda!" he cried.

She flashed a quizzical glance.

"Well, what is 'a? Took bad again, are 'e?" she asked mockingly.

The drenched flame expired in a choking smother. What was the use? He was a worm, and an immature worm at that. Let him live the fastest of lives and smoke the strongest of weeds, he could never lessen the distance that inexorable Time had set between them. If only those long-deceased parents of his had had the sense and enterprise to get married a few years sooner ! He groaned and turned his head away. Dorinda was stirred with compassion.

" Silly boy ! " she said, tenderly condescending. " Don't be so foolish as you are. I'm brave and fond of 'e, you know that ; but you're only a boy after all, and —well, there 'tis, you see."

He nodded hopelessly.

" I'll always be a sister to 'e, like," she added, with a felicitous reminiscence of Lady Enid Tremayne in the latest issue of her favourite penny story-budget.

" Sister be darned ! " he exploded, unconsciously echoing the furious moustache-gnawing Sir Jasper Maltravers in the same crimson-covered record of crime and passion.

107

"Now, Charlie dear," she coaxed, "don't 'e be so teasy with your old chum. Friendship's better than courtship, so they say."

With a violent gesture he expressed his utter disagreement with the proverbial wisdom of the ages, which indeed has few attractions for youth at any time.

"Look now, Charlie: I haven' paid 'e for those sweeties, nor I didn' mean to; but I will—there! Only mind—'tis the last time of all, and no more nonsense after this. Promise, will 'e?"

Her face was very near, with its lips like a folded clover-leaf for shape and a red clover-blossom for colour and sweetness; with its nose in the least degree tip-tilted—the kind that reminds your great poet of the petal of a flower, and your humble prose-writer of a little, impudent, graceful, cock-tailed wren; with

108

its eyes like glimpses of a sunlit autumnal wood, all brown until you gazed into them, when you found them streaked with the red of dying beech leaves and the green of fresh herbage and the grey of ash-trunks, and specked all over with points of dancing gold ; and you look deeper and deeper, and still the laughing Dryad retreats before you down avenues of colour.

"Promise, " she repeated. Unrequited calf-love resembles the stomach-ache : no pangs are fiercer or more deeply seated, yet they have never been accounted a fit subject for the tragic muse. It would take a whole treatise on aesthetics to explain why, with the best will and keenest sympathy in the world, I am unable to purge you, according to the ancient Greek prescription, with pity and terror, by exhibiting Charles Edward's flat, round, chubby face all drawn and distorted, his eyes agoggle, his mouth agape, his bosom a bear-garden of mutinous longings and tumultuous despairs. Pity that it should be so, since I foresee that never again in the course of this narrative shall we climb so near the topmost heights of passionate tragedy.

"Promise," she said for the third time, and set her lips in the sweetest of all shapes. Hard, cruel hard as her terms were, what could mortal youth do but yield? He made the signal of surrender by unaffectedly drawing the back of his hand across his mouth. A moment later, he was alone, and the world was a void, save for the vanishing after-taste of a smacking, all-too-sisterly kiss.

V

RELUCTANTLY loosing my hold for the moment on Dorinda's skirts, I invite you to accompany me through the crowd in search of Hubert. You hang back, madam, drawing together your silken skirts and shaking out the folds of your perfumed handkerchief? I assure you there is no cause for alarm, no reason to fear the least offence to any of your five most dainty senses. In all rural England you will find no crowd to compare with a crowd of Cornish merrymakers for sweetness and neatness, good looks and good humour, courtesy of behaviour and refinement of speech. Dear Cornish folk! when I dwelt among you, the dull literal Saxon in me may at times have taken offence at certain—sinuosities, shall I call them?—of your temperament. Or shall I put it that our English scale of virtues has been differently tuned and adjusted from yours, so that now and again a note would jar, just as the notes of a bagpipe, "now delicately flat, now sweetly sharp," are apt to jar on Southron ears when heard close at hand? But now, at a distance of three hundred miles and thrice three hundred days, how tunable those very discords appear—how delightful those fanciful dallyings with facts, those delicate tricks and evasions that go on in the Celtic twilight about the marble feet of the stern Rectitudes! And how your manners shine! Who so careful of the outward forms of life—the garments in which you present your souls and bodies to the world? Who so sedulous to avoid the rude and rugged aspect of things, to

trim and reverse the shabby gown, to
mitigate the harsh statement, and at all
times, in your own favourite phrase, to
turn the best side towards London.
Where else can a man frequent the company of men, and never hear an unseemly
word, or any but the most harmless and
ornamental of oaths ? Who could attain
a nicer balance of affability and reserve
in casual intercourse with the foreigner ?
How musical that soft brogue of yours,
with its unlooked-for stresses and song-like
inflexions ! Your wits, how nimble in
discourse ! Your hands and features, how
lively in narrative ! Your feelings, how instantly responsive to the call for laughter
or tears !—so that life among you is real
with the emphasized and heightened real-
ity of a stage-play in the hands of skilful
actors who never miss their cues or bungle
their points. Dear, courteous, hospitable,

sensitive folk, farmers of St. Hender and Langarrock, fishers of Pendennack and Porthvean and Tregurda, if ever I write a word in depreciation—or what you find hardest to pardon, in ridicule—of you and your ways, may I never again hear the dulcet voices of Down Along, or taste its ambrosial cream and aromatic saffron buns ; or, on its cliffs in March, feast my eyes on the snow and fire of blackthorn and gorse against the deep blue sea and bright blue sky; or in summer breathe the salt-sweet harmony of oar-weed and heather-bloom ; or feel in autumn the soft prickling caress of Atlantic rains upon my face.

We will not linger in the meadow to watch the sports committee passionately arguing out its latest award, man to man, with the unsuccessful competitors, nor even to hear the redintegrated band condescending to a purely secular polka, which it renders with all the unction and, so to speak, plantigrade sprightliness of a Baptist minister giving a humorous recitation at a penny reading. Passing out at the gate, we retrace our steps a few yards to the central square or piazza of the village, where the churchyard, the chapel, the school and the shop abut on the widened street. Here for the time the crowd is thickest; a fact which you may connect with the stir that is going on about the schoolroom door. Tea is preparing, and the accommodation is limited; it is advantageous to be among the first batch of feasters, and so secure a share in the first brewage of the pot and the first pick of the choicer cates and dainties. I look in vain for Hubert; but if you are in no hurry to find him, neither am I. Probably he is moping in some retired corner;

and if I hunted him out, I should have no choice but to do my duty and make a conscientious analysis of his confused and tattered emotions — an occupation about as profitable and entertaining as turning over a rag-bag. He is sure to pass this way before long ; meanwhile we will wait and watch the crowd.

To one figure there, conspicuous in uniform, I cannot refrain from drawing your attention, although it is of one who, I trust, will have no part to play in this blameless narrative. Yonder he stands on the chapel steps, a note-book in his hand, a furrow in his brow, his keen glance taking in every changing aspect of the scene—a sight to stir uneasy ripples on the calmest conscience, were it not an open secret that the note-book is not the official one. In him you see not merely the policeman but the journalist as well—

116

"Our Own Correspondent," in fact, to *The St. Kenna Mercury*, for St. Hender, Porthmellan, and the surrounding districts. That frown portends nothing more alarming than an anxious search after the right bit of journalese, which he pursues with the same patient ardour that no doubt he would expend on the detection of a criminal, were a criminal forthcoming. No stylist ever pondered more lovingly over the *mot juste* than he over those precious *clichés* which he marks with a cross for future reference when he meets them in the columns written by his professional brethren. Even as we watch him, his lips move, his face clears, and he hurriedly jots down some dear phrase. Is it "gay and festive scene," or "*élite* of the vicinity," or, with an ear to the distant band, "adequate rendition," or, with an eye to the welkin, "Sol in all his glory"? I know not, but the world will know next week. This I know, that the proudest, most thrilling moment of a life not unhonoured by the commendation of superintendents, was when, while watching a carnival procession, masked, torch-lit, brass-banded, the phrase "phantasmagorical pandemonium" flashed across his brain; and what veteran penny-a-liner ever bagged a plumper brace of winged words? I wave a respectful and cordial salute to a fellow-craftsman, and so leave him.

Did you ever set eyes on a better-looking crowd? Your most diligent search will hardly discover three snubbed or shapeless noses, or two underhung chins, or one tom-cat forehead. The children wear the solemn loveliness of spring flowers; the matrons are as comely as autumn itself; of the maidens I will not trust myself to speak. If physiognomy goes for anything,

then most of the elder men have missed
their vocations. Here you observe one
who should have been an ornament of the
Bench, there a possible Church dignitary,
there again an eminent actor, two or three
Harley Street surgeons, and any number
of magnificently bearded minor prophets—
all of them garbed, with the oddest air of
masquerade, in the soft black hats, black
suits, and parti-coloured neckerchiefs of the
holiday-making fisherman or farm-hand.
And the younger men are equally prepossess-
ing, in spite of their predilection for nether
garments of a livid blue, and for bowler
hats which, after the perverse nature of
their kind, always contrive to appear
either too large or too small for the heads
they cover. In passing, you note that
two distinct creases run down the back of
each trouser-leg, and you wonder by what
miracle of folding and mattress-pressure

so seemingly impossible a result has been attained.

But now, punctually on the stroke of five, the school-bell clangs, the door is thrown open, and the crowd throngs in. And here is Hubert at last, arriving just in time to see a flutter of pink-and-white skirts cross the playground and disappear. He pauses irresolute, delays for the re-tying of an already securely tied bootlace, and follows, we after him.

Every seat was already occupied, save at the farthest table, where Destiny, pur-posely as it would seem, had left two vacant places, one on Dorinda's right, the other facing her. It would have been simpler to leave only one, but that is seldom Destiny's way. Man must be given a chance to wriggle in his chains, or he might lie down and sulkily refuse to continue his part in the farce. Hubert deliberated which place he should take, and in five seconds had a dozen incontrovertible reasons for either course. Slowly he made his way behind the backs of heads, familiar and unknown, until he came to the gap opposite to where Dorinda sat. It appeared that she had not noticed his approach. There she sat, calmly eating and drinking, as cool and unconscious and inaccessibly remote as a snowy mountain peak. On the whole he thought he would remain where he was.

She lifted her cup. How genteel, how seductive the crook of that darling little finger ! She drank, as a goddess condescending to mortality might drink ; with a divine thirst, it would seem, for the cup went up and up, until the rim of it rested on the fairy bridge of her nose. And then——

Do you know what it is to encounter the challenge of two dark eyes over the edge of a tea-cup or a fan? Have you tried to decipher their enigmatic message, to "riddle what those prattling eyes would say," without the context of the other features to help you? It is a delightful but perilous experience, a fascinating but bewildering occupation. For a brief eternity of heart-beats Hubert was held enchanted; then the cup went down and the eyes with it. A sudden tide of resolution carried him round the table. It ebbed and left him stranded at the haven's mouth. Perhaps after all the other seat was preferable.

As he stood hesitant, Dorinda's hand went down and softly drew her skirt aside. His heart leapt at the shy invitation; he boldly overstepped the bench, and in the act discovered a sufficient

122

reason for both vacant places. The table
was not one, but two, set end to end at
this very spot. Above-board all was fair
and plausible, with the cloth spread over
to conceal the juncture ; but below, two
massive trestles left scant room for human
legs. He became aware that Dorinda was
shaking with suppressed laughter at the
successful springing of her little trap, and
he flushed to the roots of his hair as he
drew forth his disillusioned limb. A
quicker temper would have carried him
off in a huff ; a shade more meekness, and
he might have slunk away abashed. Being
neither an absolute hotspur nor a complete
milksop, but an average neutral compound
of the two, he remained where he was,
and attempted to insinuate himself between
the obstruction and the person seated to
the right of it. The latter, a stout, bald-
headed stranger, was too deeply occupied

with tea and cake to look up; but he
spoke aloud out of the fullness of his
mouth.

"Now-na! Don't 'e go squeezing
a tough old chap like me! Be a man
and squeeze the maid; she's young and
tender."

It was Dorinda's turn to flush, as eyes
were attracted and grins went round.
She sat up, stiff and unyielding, while
Hubert desperately inserted one rigidly
respectful leg into the vacancy. The other
remained perforce outside. His position
was anything but comfortable, but in his
present frame of mind a little physical
martyrdom did not come amiss.

A cup of bitterness was passed to him;
he took a slice of tribulation haphazard
from the nearest dish, and mechanically
gulped and chewed, staring straight in
front of him the while. If the company

thought he had any particular reason for choosing that particular seat, the company must be shown how ridiculously mistaken it was. As for the maiden, cool indifference was the most dignified as well as the easiest line to take with her.

A minute passed without event, save the accidental encounter and simultaneously hurried withdrawal of two self-conscious elbows. Then Hubert became aware that the eyes of his other neighbour were upon him. He turned, and was immediately accosted.

" One of the Hender ringers, if I ben't mistook ? Thought so. What might be the weight of that tenor bell of yourn, now ? "

" Nine hundredweight, two score and seven pound, 'a b'lieve," was the answer.

" So light as that ? Well, I was pulling to en just now, and I'd ha' set him down

for another hundred at the least. Steaming
like a crock, I was, time we rung down ;
and as for my hands—well, look for yourself. If these hands were rabbits, you'd say
they were ready for the pot, wouldn' e ? "

" We reckon that bell do take some
handling," said Hubert on the patronizing
note.

" He do that. Frame want seeing for,
I should say. Your bell ? "

" Well, no. I do mostly pull fifth."

" Hey ! 'Twas you scat the ringing
abroad just now, then ! F-ff ! You must
feel pretty and bad about en. Just as you
were walloping along like clockwork, too!
Well, well ! How did 'a happen, now ?
Heard a mazy old yarn just now, something about a maid in the belfry."

" You can believe that if you've a mind
to," said Hubert with an admirable
assumption of scorn.

" I don't, my son. Here's a good observance for 'e : Don't believe half what you'm told, and make particular inquiries about the other half. And here's another : Head o' the well for clear water. How *did* 'a happen, now ? "

" Aw, don't know. Got careless and missed my balance, s'pose."

The other regarded him with increased interest.

" Young man," he said cordially, " I'd be proud to know 'e better. For all the years I've been pulling to a bell-rope, I never heard words like those from a ringer yet. 'Touch of the cramp,' I've heard, and ' Fly got down my throat,' and fifty lies beside, so clane and round as the top of my head ; but never till this day did I hear a ringer put the fault on his own carelessness. Truth's one jewel and modesty's another, and if I was a tender

127

young maiden—spaking in a general way
and no respect to persons—I wouldn' be
so terrible quammish about being squeezed
by a honest man. 'Tidn' so often I'd get
the chance, and if ever a man deserved to
set up comfor'ble to his tay, you 'm the
one. Hoi! back oars there with they
splits!"

Forcibly capturing a convoy of buttered
buns on its way down the table, he dismissed Hubert with a friendly nod and fell
to work again.

A tiny whisper—the merest gossamer
thread of sound—caressed Hubert's left
ear.

"'Twas my fault, I fear."

He looked round into a face that was
all mournful penitence, save for the eyes,
which bade him mark the humour of the
situation. But the humour of the situation was just what he failed to see.

"I don't blame nobody," he whispered back, stiffly enough.

"Then a stone's rolled off my mind," came the pert answer.

He preserved a resentful silence.

"Thank 'e for not telling upon me," she murmured.

"I wouldn' do *that*." A whisper is by nature a colourless form of speech ; and until you have made the trial, you cannot conceive the difficulty of flushing it with the roseate hues of airy gallantry.

"If you could have seen yourself!" On her face was sketched a comic picture of imbecile astonishment—round eyes staring, mouth ajar.

"I was quite satisfied with what I did see." Nothing could be neater or apter.

"You've seen the like before, s'pose."

"Never!"

The modest eyelids drooped; unlicensed laughter twitched the bow of the lips.

"But you'm vexed at losing the prize after that."

"Not I. 'Twas worth it."

She tossed her head and coyly turned it away. This was beyond doubt or cavil the Real Thing, and she was enjoying it hugely. What next?

"How nice your hair do look, Dorinda!"

She smiled inwardly at a memory, and was tempted to try a little experiment in comparative psychology. Her hand fluttered up to her head and privily set a snare of wire.

"Shall I tell 'e a secret, Hubert?" she asked, all ingenuousness and candour. "There's thirty-five hairpins into 'n this very minute, and I do feel so complicated up top. I wonder whether you can see any sticking out or no."

His eyes strayed lingering through the magic labyrinth, and fell into the snare.

" Ess, there's one I can see."

" Would 'e mind pushing him home for me ? "

He hesitated, furtively scanning the faces of the company.

" 'Tis up under your hat to the left, " he said at length. " Where you had your hand just now."

Stupid fellow ! As if she didn't know that ! Petulantly she jabbed the pin back into its place, and pointedly she edged away from him. She knew the rules ; now was the moment, here the opportunity, for a tiff.

Dimly aware that in some unexplained manner he had lost ground, Hubert sought to retrieve it by a long stride in advance.

" I've been thinking, Dorinda, you'll

be looking for somebody to put 'e round after tay."

" You can think what you've a mind to, s'pose." It was not an encouraging answer, flung at him over the coldest of cold shoulders ; but he persevered.

" Shouldn' mind putting of 'e round myself, if you can't find nobody better," he said, on just the right note, as he flattered himself, of jaunty mock-indifference.

" 'Twould take some time to do that." He glowed. " Poor's the best of 'e." He was snuffed.

" We ben't no match for the maidens, to be sure," he rallied, and pointed the application with a meaning glance. It struck a marble stare, and fell blunted. Would a less subtle—but still subtle— compliment reach the mark ?

" Though when I consider of the maidens, seeming to me I could put my hand on the crop of the bunch, easy as I'm setting here."

He saw the contemptuous shrug of the shoulder; he could not see the involuntary smile on the averted face, nor the distracting gleam of the pearly tooth that strove to bite it in.

" Dorinda, how are you so niffy ? "

No answer, nor the least sign that she had heard him.

" If I've said anything to vex 'e——"

She turned quickly. " You couldn' do that," she flashed.

He checked an impulse to draw nearer.

" Glad to hear 'e say that," he said guardedly, as one who goes to pluck a rose with a memory of thorns in his mind.

" To vex me or plaise me, 'tis all one to me what you say," she retorted, and turned away with an air of finality.

133

Very well; final let it be. Risk another rebuff? Never, while there was manhood left in him! After all, who was she, to scorn him thus? Only little Dorinda Varco from next door. Had he not chivalrously shielded her from discovery in the belfry? Was this his reward for shouldering all the blame? Very well. His presence was distasteful to her; he would remove it as soon as might be.

He seized his neglected tea-cup and drained it to the dregs. Nauseously cold and bitter was the draught. Was all warmth and sweetness fled from the world?

A discreet elbow saluted his ribs, a husky whisper his ear.

"Honest man, did 'e ever try to catch a thistle-seed? 'Tidn' no use running after en, and the smarter you snatch to en the further 'a 'll dance away. But just you keep still, or stroll off a couple of steps, careless-like, and nine times out of ten 'a 'll come rowling after 'e and hanging to your coat-sleeve, and no brishing of it off, however you may try. Honest man, there's morals to be sarched out of thistle-seeds."

"They ben't worth the trouble of catching, anyhow," said Hubert, loud enough to be heard by anyone whom it might concern.

"My son," said the benevolent bald-head, "if you say that, I condemn 'e for a poor sportsman. 'Tidn' so much what you go forth to catch, 'tis the catching of it that count—bear that in mind. The sport's the thing. Flea or tiger, don't matter so long as 'a 'll give some sport. Nor I wouldn' spake so scornful of these thistle-seeds, nother. Pretty things, sure

135

'nough—all pluff and pilmy, and dancing along so gay and lightsome, like a maid of seventeen."

" And fine pretty weeds they grow up to," said the temporary cynic. " Preckles all over, and no getting rids of 'em, like a wife at forty."

" Well said," approved the other. " Nately took up, sure 'nough. But you'll notice the dunkey do think a brave lot of 'em ; and 'tidn' for you and me to scorn the dunkey's opinion, honest man."

At this moment a gentle tug at Hubert's coat brought the crazy walls of his castle of indifference toppling to the ground. He turned eagerly. Dorinda's eyes were on the piece of cake she was carefully crumbling in her plate. Her lips moved, and syllabled his father's name. He looked up, and there, facing them across

136

the table, towered and glowered the elder Barron. At once without premeditation, Hubert's left hand dropped to his side, and another hand, soft and small, slipped into it and clung there. And so together, like two naughty children, they awaited the stroke of doom.

During the past hour, Mr. Barron's experiences had been something like Richard Crookback's on Bosworth Field, and had left him in a similar condition of baffled fury. Three separate blazonries of pink-and-white had he marked down, pursued and confronted, only to be met on each occasion by injured innocence and a complete alibi. But now there could be no mistake. There sat the culprits, the greater and the less, in incriminating propinquity, with the consciousness of guilt writ large upon them. If the occasion was a public one, so much the worse for

137

them. He was in the mood that strikes and spares not.

"I wouldn' have believed it," he began ; and though the tones were low, they sent a stir right down the table. "The word was put into my mouth, but I spet en out agin with scorn. 'No !' I said to them, 'nobody from Sunny Corner would go to do such a thing, least of all the only cheeld of my best friend, that I've been a second uncle to all her life. Never will I believe it of her,' I said to them. And there she set ; and I'd give the world and my best hat to be able to say 'twadn' no son of mine setting next to her."

"Father ! " exclaimed Hubert with desperate vehemence.

"I'll 'tend to you presently, my son," said Nicky grimly. "Friends all," he continued, on a rising tide of oratory that swept the major part of the feasters to

138

their feet, "some of 'e do know me and some don't. They that do know me do know me for one that don't know the maning of fear nor yet of favour. Soon 's I see roguery I go for 'n——don't matter who 'tis or where 'tis. Do I take credit by that? No. 'Tis my nature——can't help myself ; 'tis my duty——wouldn' help myself if I could."

On an effective pause he gathered his audience with his eye. The deathlike silence was broken by a murmured comment from the bald-headed unknown.

" " 'Tis my nature *and* my duty,' said the mad bull ; and up went the old woman, tiss-toss, sky-high."

Without catching the words, Nicky recognized the hostile nature of the interruption, and went for the interrupter with your practised orator's readiest weapon.

"Tell 'e what, my man ; if I hadn'

got more sense than hair, and none o'
that to spake of, I'd keep my mouth
shut."

"Well put in," muttered the stranger
with a grin, and pensively rubbed the spot
where the bludgeon had fallen.

"Now, friends," resumed Nicky, "you
d' all know the onmerited disgrace that
have been put upon we ringers of St.
Hender in our own church tower this day.
'Tidn' for me to say our set's well known
for the best set in this locality, nor I won't
say we never yet missed first prize without the jedges had their own li'll bit of
bacon to fry ; but our name's well up, 'a
b'lieve, and I think you'll agree that our
place an't the bottom place at all and
not even a hon'rable mention to save
our credit. But that's our place to-day.
And how ? Where's the saycret cause
and raison thereof ? Where's the brass-

face piece of female mischief that geeked
in and distorted my onfortunate son's
attention, and scat to flatters as pretty a
touch as ever was rung in Hender tower?
There!" Out shot his accusing fore-
finger. "There she sit before me, peck-
ing up bread-crumbs like a innocent li'll
sparrer, more shame to her, and let her
deny it if she dare take the chance of the
next crumb choking her!"

He ended on a trumpet-note, dominant
over the rising uproar of feet and voices.
I despair of doing justice to the scene—
the pallid couple sitting mute, hand in
hand; their accuser fixed like a statue in
the attitude of denunciation; the excited
revellers pressing about them, gloating,
vociferating, clambering on benches, even
mounting the tables, to the imminent
peril of the crockery. Suddenly at the
door the hubbub swelled still louder, and

fiery, far-seen, like the oriflamme of France, the meteor-beard of Dickon Varco clove the press. With a sharp question or two he mastered the situation as he went ; and when he took up his position confronting Nicky, with a protecting hand on Dorinda's shoulder, the light of battle glowed baleful in his eye.

On a sudden hush the duel began.

"Now, Nick Barron, what's all this foolishness ? "

"Dick Varco, I warn 'e, best not inter- fere 'twixt me and my duty."

"Duty ! Pretty sort of duty, bully-rag- ging my daughter at a public tay ! "

"When I see roguery——"

"Roguery ! I'll trouble 'e not to put that word 'pon my flesh and blood ! "

"I put my words where they belong. I got the proofs. Didn' she geek in——"

"Tshutt! You d' talk sick. What if she did? Bit of harmless cur'osity, same as any maid's liable to, summer-time. Where's your roguery there? What for should the cheeld want to upsot you and your gashly old tin pots and brass pans, I'd like to know?"

"Tin pots! Take care, Dickon Varco! Brass pans! Ah! 'tidn' the first time you've scandalized our bells, nor yet the second. 'Only Dickon's quips,' said I, and went on trusting of 'e—called 'e my best friend only this minute. But now my eyes be opened, and I see—ah, what do I see?"

"Can tell 'e that aisy, b'lieve. Slap through the millstone and into the mare's nest—that's of it, Nicky-Nick-Nick!"

"I see a rat-hole, and I smell a black-hearted old rat crumped up inside of it, scratching his red whiskers and planning a

143

roguery that he don't dare put a hand to himself. But here's the young rat handy. ' Pst, my dear ! Go to so-and-so and do so-and-so. One of my celebrated little jokes, you know.' ' All right, daddy.' ' Tie up your tail first, my dear, so they shan't reco'nize 'e.' ' So I will, daddy,'— and off she go, tie her tail in a knot, and —fah ! Harmless cur'osity ? No ! A cooked job, by goles ! "

Dickon's anger was ebbing fast. He threw his hands abroad with a gesture of humorous despair.

" My life ! Here's a smother and a smeech of a damp straw bonfire ! Here's a toddy old Fifth of November yarn spinned out of a lock of dirty cobwebs ! Some brains do want a broom took to 'em, I reckon."

" And some backs do want a broom-stick took to 'em ! There's for you,

Dickon Varco ! Yes, I name 'e for what you are—a black-hearted, white-livered, red-whiskery varmin ! "

At this polychromatic insult the assembly burst into renewed uproar. Shouts of ironical laughter, of stern reprobation, of friendly admonition, were showered on the combatants. Dickon marked the frenzy of his old friend's eye, the trembling of his outstretched fist ; and the last spark of resentment died down within him.

" Come, Nicky, old comrade," he said earnestly, " this won't do. I'm sorry now, and you'll be sorry directly. Looksee— I take back every word I've said, and there's my hand."

" Never ! I've done with 'e for good and all, hand-shake and mouth-speech, from this time henceforth till we're both in our graves."

"Fare 'e well, then," said Dickon, not without dignity. "Till burying-time so be it. But I'll be looking for 'e to make it up, come Jedgment Day," he added with a twinkle, as he drew Dorinda to her feet and started for the door.

Nicky's parting shot was unanswered, and, for his credit's sake, shall remain unrecorded.

VI

OUTSIDE in the sunshine, the father drew his daughter's arm closer within his own, and soothed her agitation with a few reassuring pats, but for the present said no word, wise and considerate parent that he was. Passing out of the playground, they came upon Mr. Roscorla, stranded by some unknown mischance in the middle of the road. His wizard ash was tracing magic circles in the dust, of its own volition, apparently ; he looking on with the corrugated forehead and pursed-up lips of one who curiously and doubtfully investigates some strange phenomenon of Nature. What subtle instinct warned him of Dorinda's approach, that even as he looked up he was already struggling into a smile as into a heavy overcoat ? What power, as he opened his broad-beaming mouth to speak, breathed into it the inspiration of a lifetime ?

"Fine courting weather for the chaps," he croaked, with the sly triumphant look of the chess-player who forestalls his opponent's move. To his utter amazement the answer came, not in words or in laughter, but in a sudden torrent of tears. In another moment a bristling embodiment of wrath, impossible to recognize as the easy-going Dickon, had swept him aside with a push that was almost a blow, and the two were gone, leaving him to reconstruct the universe as best he might out of the boiling mists of chaos.

"Stupid old bufflehead !" growled Dickon. "Clumsy g'eat foot, stanking 'pon my poor li'l tender worm ! Come,

stiddy's the word, my lovely! Stiddy,
then! Sun gone black out with 'e, have
'um? Not a bit of it; only a trumpery
li'l cloud got in the way of 'm for a
minute. Why "—he cocked an eye overhead—" if I do live, there 'a be all the
while; ess, there's bright Phœbus shining
up aloft like a good one! Shine up, old
cap'n! Here's the dew 'pon a rose-bush
want drying."

Not the words, but their miserable
inadequacy as a means of consolation,
faintly stirred her inherited sense of
humour. She smiled wanly through her
tears, and blindly fumbled at her belt.

" Lost handk'cher? Take mine,
cheeld," said Dickon, whipping out a
small crimson table-cloth. " Lost or
found, you'll never sop up all that wet
with yourn. These female go-to-meeting
handk'chers are like a weathercock in a

lew—more ornyment than use. Come,
better now? That's right; and the eyes
of 'e all the brighter for their sprinkling,
I'll be bound. Lev us see to 'em. Ah!
bright as a bush-sparrow's. Take 'em
out and hang 'em to your ears, my pretty,
and where'll the Queen's diments be
then?"

His tender nonsense began to have its
calculated effect.

"Silly old daddy!" she dimpled, with
a little push of reviving coquetry.

"At your sarvice, my dear," he chuck-
led. "Dickon Varco, raisonable old and
terrible silly, sure enough, but no bad
hand to a compliment after that, as your
ma 'll bear witness. Many 's the one
I've paid her in the old ancient days.
To tell 'e the truth, that bit about the
diments was one of 'em; I can mind to
his day how she paid me back for 'm

with a slap 'cross the face, and brave and proud I was of the favour. A smack was counted most the same as a kiss, they days. Cur'ous how matrimony do change a man's convictions ! "

Dorinda turned an incredulous eye on the dim past. No ; loving and dutiful daughter though she was, she could not summon up a plausible picture of father showering jewelled compliments on mother, and mother requiting him with kittenish pats. Yet so it must have been ; hard as it was to realize, all these staid middle-aged folk had certainly been young once upon a time. The logical corollary of this novel reflection took the horrid form of a nightmare glimpse into the far future, where she and a not impossible he sat chained together, two stout and grizzled ghosts, indifferent and unthrilled, in a shadowy kitchen over a spectral fire that warmed not. She shivered violently, and her eyes brimmed over anew.

"Why, Dorinda——" Dickon began with anxious concern.

"Take me home!" she cried, clinging to him. "Oh, I wish I was dead! Take me home, daddy!"

"There, there!" he soothed her. "Nerves all abroad, and no wonder. What you want is a nice quiet set-down for half an hour somewhere out of the way with nobody to plague 'e. And here's the very place, where I was taking you to all the time. Feast-day or worky-day, fair or foul, don't matter how 'tis with us outside, 'tis always Sunday arter-noon in to Aunt Jenny Hosken's."

So saying, he steered her unresisting, poor storm-tossed pleasure-boat that she was, through a garden gate, up between ranks of happy neglected roses, under a porch embowered in cool-haired creepers, and so into the harbourage of a tiny low-ceiled kitchen, sweet and still and exquisitely ordered, where nothing stirred save a spot of sunlight quietly dancing with its attendant shadows on the wall.

Deep in an arm-chair slumbered a small, frail old lady, with the rarest, sweetest face that was ever carved out of old ivory and tinged with the hue—"less than of roses, more than of violets"—of the blossoming orchard. The son of Sirach once saw such another, and compared its beauty to the clear light upon the holy candlestick. Time appears to mankind in many shapes, most of them forbidding enough ; looking on Aunt Jenny's face, you could picture him in the most amiable of aspects, as a cunning craftsman of a primitive age, squatting

153

down before an ordinary piece of mortal
clay, and slowly and patiently elaborating
it into a quaint and exquisite work of art,
fining away the mere superfluities of flesh,
bringing out, touch by touch, the intrinsic
humanity that lay beneath, and hatching
and raying and fretting all the surface
with a delicate tracery of innumerable fine
lines, and never a line misplaced or too
deeply bitten, to spoil the serenity with
a suggestion of trouble or discontent.

Mr. Varco, standing at delighted gaze
in the doorway, paid his tribute of
admiration in simpler coin, none the less
adequate, I dare say, for that.

" Aw, the old dear av 'um ! " he whispered. " Beat the waxworks holler,
don't 'a ? "

At the sound of his voice she awoke,
suddenly and completely, as old folk do ;
and two eyes of a dim radiance looked

straight into Dorinda's out of an immeasurable past. It has a singular effect, this first momentary look of an old person just fetched back from her other world of dreams. Surprise is not there, nor recognition, nor any human emotion, but a sort of impersonal dispassionate judgment, not very easy for a mortal with a conscience to endure.

The moment passed, and a gently smiling, softly garrulous old dame was warmly welcoming her guests. The forms of greeting and personal inquiry having been dispatched, Dickon took up a newspaper which lay on the table at Aunt Jenny's elbow, with her spectacles beside it.

" Any news 'pon the paper, I wonder ? " said he, and plunged haphazard into a column.

" Hullo ! " he exclaimed at once.

"'New Year concert at Polskiddy'?" His eyes sought the top of the page. "Why, aunty, if I do live, you've got hold of a paper six months old."

"I know, my dear," she replied placidly. "You see, 'tis this way. Boy Albert, he's a rare one for the news, and he get the paper every week reg'lar, and when he've done with en he put en by for me. There's a wonderful lot of good news 'pon the paper every week, and I can't bear to miss none of it ; but I ben't much of a scholar, my dears, and then agin my eyes an't what they used to be. So there 'tis ; the new paper do come along before I've finished up with the old one, and that's how I've come to drop behind-hand a bit. Don't suppose I'll ever catch up agin, not in this world. But there, my dears !—I reckon all news be fresh news when you haven' heard en before."

" That's so sure 'nough," agreed Dickon.
" Or if 'tidn' azackly fresh, 'tis thereafter,
as the fish-jowster said for the mackerel."

" Besides, my dears," she continued,
" this old news, I do find en more comfortable, like, than if 'a was raw-new.
There's a dreadful accident, then, 'pon
the paper you got in your hand ; a rail-
way accident, my dears—six poor sinners
sent to their 'count, and five-and-twenty
wownded. If that had happened the day
before yes'day, and I'd come to hear of
'en, 'twould be more than I could bear,
to think upon the poor m'urning wives
and cheldern, and the suffering souls 'pon
their beds up to hospital, and the doctors
with their gashly g'eat knives a-cutting
of 'em up. But seeing 'tis all over and
done with months ago—tears dried, proper
new headstones put up 'pon the graves,
wownds stitched up, handsome wooden

157

legs provided for them that do require them—why, it do just touch the heart softly, like when you call to mind your own sorrows back-along."

" Ah ! " said Dickon, sympathetically leading her on, " all the world do know you've had a sight of trouble in your time, aunty."

" Trouble and joy, my dears, trouble and joy. The sour and the sweet ; couldn' be other, could 'a ? Nor you wouldn' have it other when you'm old like me, and think more 'pon what's past than you do 'pon what's to come. 'Tis like when you set down to supper after your day's work, and look for a bit of a relish to your bread. The jam and the pickles, my dears—the sweet and the sour ; there they be 'pon table, and you fit and spread the one or the other, according as you have a mind to."

" Hear that, cheeld ? " said Dickon. "Jam and pickles—a tasty li'l parable, sure enough. Aunty, here's a maid been trying her hand to a two-pound jar this very arternoon, and 'twadn' no jam nother."

Aunty nodded with an infinite knowingness.

" My old eyes ben't so wake but what I could see that, soon as you come in," she said. " Look, my lovely, I wonder if you could fancy giving a old woman a kiss."

If Dorinda hung back for a moment, her excuse is to be found in the natural reluctance of healthy youth to participate in anything of the nature of a sentimental scene. It was only for a moment. Dickon was a charmed spectator of a pretty tableau of youth and age sheltering together, cheek by cheek, in a soft shower of summer rain. As he confessed afterwards, it strained his buttons considerable.

The slamming of the garden gate, followed by the sound of a hurried step on the path, dissolved the picture and sent Dorinda whisking back to her seat. As the steps came nearer, a high-pitched voice was heard ejaculating broken phrases.

" No use . . . Can't please 'em nohow . . . Wearing out my new shoes . . . Might so well give up to once."

" 'Tis boy Albert !" cried the old lady in some agitation. " What's brought en home so soon, I wonder ? "

In at the door plunged a short, scrubby, middle-aged man, with a moustache like an age-worn, time-stained tooth-brush, and eyes that resembled ice marbles in a state of incipient liquefaction. His attire was of a composite nature, something after the fashion of those figures in a child's toy-

book in which the head, body, and legs
are interchangeable. A blue peaked cap
was superimposed on a black tail-coat and
fancy waistcoat, and those again on tight
white flannel trousers and white canvas
shoes ; so that, looking him over from
head to foot, you began your acquaintance
with the mate of a coasting vessel, went
on to a small country tradesman at a tea-
party, and finished up with a cricketer
arrayed for the field.

"No good, mother! Missed my chances
agin," he began, before he was momentarily checked by the sight of the visitors.

"My poor boy!" quavered Aunt Jenny,
all tender brooding concern.

"I've tried brown boots," he complained,
after nodding shortly to Dickon and
peering curiously at Dorinda as she
sat by the window with her back to
the light. "I've tried white shoes. I've

tried fancy waistcoats and plain ones. I've made the experiment of a box-hat. I've gone beyond my means in neckties. No good. Young maidens, old maidens, widow women—not one of 'em will so much as look upon me sideways. Fine raiment, conversational abilities, generous disposition about the cash, moral character beyond investigation—what mo re th ey want I can't think for my life. But it all goes for nothing in their sight. If I should look to have a chance, there's always another fellow got the priority. Aw, Bethesda ! "

" It's a shame for them ! " twittered his mother indignantly. " The best son that ever was ! Who be they to scorn him, I'd like to know ? "

" I'm a travelled man," he pursued, un-ostentatiously manœuvring for an inspection of Dorinda's profile. " I've been to

Mexico, and I've been to Gloucester. I've invested my money in liabilities like a gentleman, and passed through the insolvency court without a stain on my credit. I've got literature, and I've had profitable convictions of sin. What more do they want ?—that's where I'm puzzled to."

"True, my dears," Aunt Jenny chimed in, while her son carelessly edged himself window-wards, so as to get the light on Dorinda's back hair. "True every word of it. And what's more, when he give his mind to it, his equal for polishing brass candlesticks and smoking out bee-hives an't to be found in the land. And that gentle and consedrate to his old mother——"

"That'll do, mother ; you needn' chatter so. If I have got the domestic qualifications, you can leave them under the bushel where I keep them to. By all accounts, they don't go for much in the female estimation. A spice of the devil— ah! that's where the vacancy's to, or I'm sadly mistaken. If only—but there! 'twas left out of me at birth, more's the pity. No blame to you, mother, nor to father neither. You did your best for me between you, but I do wish there'd been a touch of rampageousness somewhere in the family: just enough to flavour me up, if you understand, without risking my spiritual welfare. But no; 'tisn't in me, not so much as a speckle. And if you haven't got the seed, how are you going to cultivate the blossom?" he plaintively inquired, stooping a little to peep under the brim of Dorinda's hat.

"Ah!" sighed Dickon, all sympathy. "I knowed a man once whose case was the very spit of yourn. Good looks, manners of a lord, every merit, heart and pocket both, and never a kind word could that man get out of the maidens, all for the want of a ha'porth of rakishness. 'A did his best to improve himself too : tried the drink, and the drink made him sick ; tried profane language and desolate company, but the bad words sticked to the teeth of 'm like tar, and as for the low companions, they scorned to consort with him ; if he'd been a lay preacher, they couldn' have scorned him more. A hopeless case, sure enough. Ah, poor chap !"

" What became of him ? " asked the other with nervous anxiety.

" Well, by what I've been told, the crowner—but I'd rather not tell 'e, if you don't mind. Don't wish to upset the ladies. 'A was about your height too, I reckon, but a bit bigger 'pon the round before 'a begun to waste away."

" Tell 'e what 'tis," exclaimed Albert

with gloomy emphasis. "It won't be long before I do something rash myself. 'Tisn't to be borne with, particularly holiday time, with all the rest of the world sorted out fit for the Ark, and me going about on my singular perambulations, till I'm ashamed to show my face in the street."

"Cheer up," said Dickon consolingly. "Think upon your merits. Cheap clome's aisy to match ; but when you come to a best Crown Derby parlour ornyment, it take some sarching to make up the pair."

"There's that to consider of, certainly," mused Albert, brightening a little. "And I've been thinking, maybe I'm too profligate with my favours. Easy got, little valued, and the free sample do go upon the dust-heap so often as not. If I should hold off a bit more, now—a touch of fustigiousness, as you may say. And I fancy whether it would be advisable to change back to my grey trousers against the evening . . . What do the young lady think ? " he asked, abruptly addressing Dorinda.

Dorinda gave him a full view of the demurest of faces, and soberly opined that Mr. Albert looked beautiful as he was.

" Ah ! " said Mr. Albert, staring at her with bulging eyes. Suddenly he turned, drew Dickon into a corner, and whispered an anxious inquiry behind his hand.

" Not that I know by," replied Dickon aloud. " There was a chap, a staid man with a bit of property ; but he 've been turned off for light behaviour, 'a b'lieve."

A still more urgent whisper followed.

" Don't know but what she might," said Dickon. " We 'll ask her."

" One moment," said Albert, detaining

167

him for a further and longer communication, as full of vehement sibilants as a nest of angry adders. Its import was dimly discernible by the light of Dickon's answers.

" I see. . . Azackly so—just a prelim'ry canter, like . . . No, wouldn' think of holding 'e to en. . . . Yes, best make it clear to her. . . . Very well, I'll tell her."

The colloquy coming to an end, Mr. Varco advanced towards his daughter, ceremoniously leading Albert by the breast-lapel of his coat. If it had been by the lobe of his ear, he could not have looked more sincerely undignified.

" Dorinda, my cheeld," said her parent, with a solemn visage on which the faintest of winks flickered for a moment and vanished, " I should like to recommend to your notice Mr. Albert Hosken, who wish to know if you'd be disposed to walk round with him this evening, 'pon trial, like. He don't wish to bind himself to nothing, nor have nothing brought up agin him hereafter by way of ser'ous intentions, if so be you don't come up to the mark 'pon further acquaintance. But 'a do like the looks of 'e terrible well, and there an't no telling what might happen if you behave conformable. What do 'e say, my dear ? "

" Ready to do everything that's proper," subjoined the suitor, putting such a strain on his eyeballs that there really seemed a danger of their plopping out on the floor. " Would go so far as eighteen-pence for expenses, or even two shillings 'pon occasion, share and share alike, and barring the merry-go-round, which is apt to take me with a squeamishness upon the chest. Well stored with interesting information to keep the conversation going,

169

and would undertake to wash my hands
or put on my kid gloves, whichever you
please, in case you want to take my
arm."

"There's for 'e !" exclaimed Mr. Varco
with enthusiasm. "Nobody couldn' say
fairer than that."

"Do 'e now, my dear !" urged Aunt
Jenny. "Only give him a trial; a fair
trial's all he want. Just to plaise his old
mother, my dear."

All eyes were on Dorinda, as she sat
struggling to keep her features in decent
order against the stress of some obscure and
powerful emotion. Perhaps it was mere
wickedness ; perhaps it was the reflection
that the least eligible of cavaliers is better
than no cavalier at all ; perhaps, as I like
to think, it was an impulse of pity for the
odd figure standing before her with every
muscle astrain on the agonizing rack of

expectation, that induced her at last to murmur a modest and guarded assent.

"Just a minute while I fetch my cane with the silver top," said Albert, precipitating himself towards the staircase door ; while his mother began to babble happily of the merits of the best son that ever was, confessing by the way that her dearest wish was to see him well started on the matrimonial path before the time came for her to leave him alone in the world.

"For he an't one to get along by himself, my dears. Leave alone the churrs and the cookery, he's bound to have somebody to talk to in the house, or he'd fall into a decline. There ain't a more scopious talker nowheres than boy Albert ; and no trouble at all to listen to en, for 'a don't look for no answering back, most of the while. Sometimes, my dears——"

Aunt Jenny dropped her voice and confidentially tapped the side of her nose—"sometimes after supper I should close my eyes for ten minutes or a quarter of an hour—might be longer at a particular time ; but so long as I don't go so far as downright snoring, he don't notice nothing; and when I come to wake up agin, there he is, discoursing away. And good solid stuff, mind 'e—none of your fullish quips and randy tales. The Lord be thanked, my boy never made a joke in his life."

"There an't many you could say so much for," said Dickon. "Seeming to me, Dorinda, you'm a lucky maid."

"Mind 'e, my dear," continued Aunt Jenny, quivering an impressive finger at Dorinda, "he's a bit particular in some of his ways—wouldn't be a man if 'a wadn'. Now if you'll look 'pon the dresser behind 'e, you'll see a cup—a breakfas' cup, my

172

dear, all alone by himself beside the sugar-basin."

Dorinda looked.

" 'Tis a very dirty cup," she said, with a *moue* of disgust. " Haven't been washed for weeks, by the looks of it."

" Weeks ! " exulted the old lady. " My dear, I give 'e my word, 'tis more 'n two year since that cup was streamed! 'Tis my boy's cup, the one he drink his cocoa out of, for tay he never could abide, calling it lappy trade with no nature into 'n ; nor I don't deny but what cocoa's the more ser'ous beverage of the two, as he do say, though to my mind 'a must be mortal disturbing to the stomick when you take it so thick as he do, and no telling what to call en, food or drink. But there 'tis : all sorts of appetites in the world, and I don't doubt but our insides be so deffrant one from another as our outsides, if we could

173

get to see them.   But we can't, my dears ;
thanks be, we can't do no such thing.
Now about the cup, my dears : one evening he took a fancy 'bout the cocoa tasting of paraffin, and I won't say but what
'a might ha' been so ; for the maid that
help me about the house, she's a good
little maid, but a bit careless in and out,
partic'lar when she've been changing her
sweetheart, and I allow 'tis aisy to mistake
your clouts when you 'm thinking over
what he said and what you said ; but any-
ways, boy Albert he up and declare that
if the cup couldn' be claned proper 'a
shouldn' be claned at all ; and what's
more,' a *haven'* been claned from that day
to this ; and that 'll show 'e how nice and
partic'lar my boy is.   But hoosh !—here
'a do come."

. Not only had he fetched his cane and
donned his gloves of purple kid, but he

had made considerable alterations in the rest of his attire. The grey trousers had carried the day after all; the head-gear was now of straw, flamboyantly beribboned; and while the tail-coat remained, the waistcoat, by a touch of foppish negligence worthy of Brummel himself, had been discarded altogether, so as to give the pale blue braces and the pink-and-gold necktie the prominence they deserved.

" Now, miss, if you're ready," he announced, " we'll leave the old people to themselves and proceed upon our itiner'y."

" Old people ! " Dickon's beard went up. " Say, Albert, do 'e mind minching from school and robbing Farmer Olver's orchard, you and me together, and the old man coming along and poking us down with his ox-goad ? My life, how you did yowl and skip ! "

175

Albert stared blankly, wondering, no doubt, whither this putid and irrelevant fable tended.

"No recollection," he said shortly. "Never made myself ridiculous in my life. Must have been some other person. If you're ready, miss."

VII

ONCE in the garden, Mr. Hosken wasted
no time in trifling with brown bread
and anchovies, but proceeded at once to
the solid dishes. He had been giving his
mind, it appeared, to the political situation,
which was stirring his gravest anxiety.
The superfluous behaviour of both Houses
was such, he declared, as wouldn't be
tolerated for a moment on a parish
council. The conduct of the Peers came
in for special condemnation; he was
credibly informed that instead of attend-
ing to the business of the nation they
were supinely content to stay at home in
their drawing-rooms, where they wallowed
about in their shirt-sleeves, drinking iced
lemonade. Parliament House was burnt

down in 1834 ; the amount of insurance,
if any, was unknown to him. He had
seen the London firemen in their uni-
forms : noble brass helmets, something
like those worn by the horse-soldiers, but
lacking feathers. Feathers, as Dorinda
would understand, were not suitable for
firemen, being liable to inflammation.
Speaking of feathers—— In parenthesis
Dorinda was requested to hold on ; they
wouldn't meet anybody if they went up
that side-turning ; and where was the
advantage in walking together if they
didn't make a proper exhibition of themselves ? And would she mind stepping a
bit slower, or they wouldn't have wind
enough for their dialogue. About feathers,
he was going to say——

But Dorinda was already yawning without concealment ; and although, for my
part, I had rather be bored to extinction

in her company than be madly entertained elsewhere, I am not sufficiently assured of your feelings to risk the experiment on your patience. So we will fall back a yard or two, if you please, and await events. You might easily be less agreeably employed than in walking along behind a pretty country girl who is accustomed to carry pitchers of water from the well and pails of butter-milk to the pigs, and so has kept up her childish practice in balancing herself on her feet—that plainsong of motion, which her town-bred sisters either neglectfully drawl over, like sleepy choristers, or else disfigure with fancied descants—too florid mincings and writhings. Freed from the compulsion of her eyes, you will have a better opportunity of observing the poise of her head, sensitive and sprightly as a bird's or a flower's. Now and then, as she looks aside, you

will be favoured with an unfamiliar view
of her face—a quarter-view, with her nose
marvellously appearing and disappearing
beyond the round of her cheek, as a
fishing-boat's one sail comes into sight and
vanishes over a distant wave. You will
follow, with little hindrance from puff and
frill and flounce, that most exquisite series
of lines which begins about her ear and
slopes down with ever-varying curve and
crankle to the hem of her skirt. You will
dwell as long as you dare on the slender—
not too slender—waist, and wish that the
epithet "buxom" had not been despoiled of
its right old meaning by clumsy mishand-
ling. You will cast one respectful glance
at the ankles, and refrain, as you value
your peace of mind, from casting a second.

And beside her goes a much-too-long-
tailed coat, topped with a quite unrelated
straw hat, and borne along on two short

and agitated legs, which now stretch into a stride, now break into a trot, as they valiantly attempt to keep pace with one whose steps are tuned each moment to a higher pitch of impatient boredom. And ever the scrannel voice toils on, indefatigably ranging the whole gamut of human knowledge in search of some chord that may arrest the feminine attention and touch the feminine heart.

They turned into the main street, and Dorinda had cause to remember that recent events had made her a notorious young person, and also to realize that her present escort did not diminish her conspicuousness. The stares of the old were hard to endure ; harder the sniggers of the young. She grew desperate, meditating flight ; but how run from the cockleburr that has hooked itself to your gown ? Would no one deliver her ?

She saw Charles Edward approaching ;
but—oh, the fickleness of youth !—he was
not alone.   Red-cheeked, uneasily smirk-
ing, he walked beside a many-flounced,
black-browed, high-coloured siren of his
own age.   He did not even see her as he
passed.   A little farther on, Mr. Roscorla
hove into sight ; but no Dutch canal-boat
was less adapted than he for a cutting-out
expedition, even if he had not been
moored fast to his vigilant sister, and hopelessly hemmed in by a whole flotilla of
cackling women-folk.

Now her heart gave a great thump, as
Hubert Barron swung into view up street.
Here at last came the gallant knight to
rescue her from this goggle-eyed paste-
board dragon.   He drew near ; she hoisted
every available signal of distress.   He saw
her, and checked his progress.   His glance
fell on her companion ; he curled a bitter

smile of reproachful scorn, and hastened by with averted head.

She had long since ceased to pay any attention to the muddy gutter of talk that flowed by her elbow, but now her notice was drawn by its sudden stoppage on an interrogatory note.

"Plaise?" she said indifferently.

"Should value your particular opinion on the subject," said Albert earnestly.

"What subject?" she was prompted by a faint stir of curiosity to ask.

"Why, miss, Australia, to be sure! Tasmania's all right, and so's New Zealand, but I've got my misgivings about Australia, as I said. Some say island, some again say continent, and, seeming to me, 'tis a thing that ought to be properly cleared up for educational purposes. What do you think about it?"

"Don't think about it at all," said

Dorinda wearily. "How don't 'e go there and see for yourself?"

"Go there and see?" Albert fingered his chin over this unexpected suggestion. "No good, miss," he decided. "You see —if you'll kindly give me your attention——"

She withdrew her attention, as the gutter spouted anew. Would no one deliver her?

A rakish-looking craft was discerned, hovering to the windward. A brief fire of sidelong glances was exchanged, a red flag fluttered, and the pirate ranged alongside.

"Oh, Harry! Laura turned 'e off already?"

"Seemingly so. We had a few words about somebody."

"Somebody?"

"Prettiest maid to Hender Feast."

184

DORINDA'S BIRTHDAY

Here again I am tempted to make use of a pretty old word which has been unjustly degraded from its place among the poets' toys. If George Herbert could make the conscious stars in heaven simper ; if Herrick could apply the same expression to the modest blush on an apple's cheek ; why should I be debarred from employing it to denominate the rosy twinkling coyness of my heroine ? Boldly, then, let me declare that it was with a simper that Dorinda replied—

" Who's that, I wonder ? "

" I know, and so do you, I reckon."

His bold looks scorched her cheek and troubled her breathing. Harry Laity's reputation was no secret ; there was not a mother in Porthmellan and St. Hender but time and again had solemnly warned her daughters against this too handsome young fisherman with the sleepy eye and the loose-lipped mouth. How much real harm there was in Harry I am not prepared at this juncture to say ; but in any case I think Dorinda may be trusted to keep out of actual mischief; and you must be very hard-hearted if you would deny her the tremulous delight of venturing a little way on the thin ice beyond the danger signal. There are excuses for her in plenty—Harry's good looks ; the anticipated zest of taking a hand in the game of games against a notoriously skilful adversary ; the pressing need of getting rid of one admirer ; the desire, perhaps, of requiting another of his scorn—all these are warrantable motives in village streets as in urban ball-rooms.

Meanwhile Mr. Albert Hosken was shifting from foot to foot like a cat on a hot slab, and adjusting and readjusting his necktie and braces in a manner expressive of the utmost impatience and apprehension.

"Come, miss," he broke in at last. "Time to accelerate our itiner'y."

Harry Laity surveyed him deliberately from head to foot.

"What's this?" he asked with cool insolence.

"'Tis a man, b'lieve," giggled Dorinda.

"Want a bit more baking, don't 'a?" drawled Harry. "Put in with the dough and took out with the cakes, I reckon."

"Go you along, young feller!" puffed Albert.

"Well," said Harry, "if I did have to pawn my waistcoat, at least I'd button my coat 'fore go out."

"Young feller, go you along!" repeated Albert, visibly shaking, while Dorinda burst into a rather shrill and prolonged laugh, which soared and quivered

like a climbing skylark. And as the song
of the dropping skylark does not die on a
cadence as others do, but is abruptly cut
off in the middle of a phrase as the bird
nears the ground, so Dorinda's laughter
was checked and cut off as she found herself being quietly led away with her arm
tucked under Harry's.

Stupefaction held Albert rooted for a
moment ; the next, he was in flustered
pursuit.

"Young feller, she's bespoke ! Miss,
you're under contract for the evening—
two witnesses, proper shape and form !
Miss, miss ! I hold 'e answerable—loss
of time, soiled gloves, damaged feelings.
Young feller, I'm a patient vessel, but I
give 'e warning——"

Harry halted and wheeled about.

"Ess ? What's your 'noyance ?" he
asked amiably.

"No offence, mister," said Albert, inching back a pace. "Nor no blame to you, not knowing the facts. If you'll give me your attention——"

"You wouldn' be disposed to fight, s'pose?" said Harry with ominous affability.

"No offence, old chap. Speaking as one man to another, I've always set a valiant face agin personal bloodshed, leave alone being the only support of my mother, an aged and timmersome person who do adore me. But when it come to the facts——"

"You won't fight, then?"

"Never while I've the spirit of a man in me," said Albert firmly. "But when I give 'e the facts, that's where your eyes 'll be opened. Now this young female——"

"Looksee," said Harry, with the air of one who makes a generous concession, "you keep the facts to yourself, and I'll keep the maid to myself. That's fair enough, 'a b'lieve. So long, old cap'n."

"Miss!" exclaimed Albert with a last despairing appeal. "With regard to the expenses, if I should guarantee up to half a crown net——"

They looked back over their shoulders : Dorinda with a pitiless smile and head-shake, Harry with a contemptuously good-natured injunction to run home-along to his ma before he got hurted ; and Albert was left forlorn and lamenting.

"No good! Missed my chance again!" he soliloquized out of an abyss of dejection, and looked about for a button to cling to.

A very small and sticky urchin was seated on a neighbouring doorstep, patiently endeavouring to coax a shy half-penny through the slit of a money-box with the aid of a jam-besmeared table-knife. There is no occupation more engrossing than the pursuit of wealth, and its deadening effect on the human sympathies is notorious; but the note of anguish in Albert's voice would have pierced the churlish absorption of a Daniel Dancer. The juvenile capitalist desisted from his efforts to realize, and with suspended knife stared open-mouthed at Albert, who needed no further encouragement to make him the recipient of his gloomy confidences.

"That settles it, my son; I give up. Odd man out—that's my tally to my dying day, if I live so long; and if another flood should come along, where'd I be? Might so well go and drown myself in advance. Ah yes! Mark my words, old chap, that's what 'twill come to before long —trumpery insanity and a rash act in a

mud-pool, or else with a clothes-line if
more convenient at the time, and the
sooner the better. Tell 'e what, my son ;
you'd best hide up that knife before I do
something desperate 'pon the spot."

Unexpectedly taking him at his word,
Albert's youthful auditor gathered his be-
longings to his bosom and hurried within
doors. Once more Albert was left alone
in an unsympathetic world. After a moment's melancholy reflection, he slowly
elevated his right leg, bending it in front
of him as he did so, until the outside of
the foot rested against the other leg a
little way above the knee. Having attained this position, he carefully steadied
himself with the aid of the cane with the
silver top, and attempted to examine the
sole of his foot. The exploit, not without its difficulties for a long-legged man,
approaches the impossible in the case of

one built on the model of a dachshund. Clutching the foot with his disengaged hand, Albert managed to drag it into a position more convenient for inspection ; but the effort impaired his equilibrium; the treacherous cane bent beneath his weight, and after one or two stork-like hops he was constrained to become a biped once more. But he had seen enough to confirm his worst forebodings.

" New last week," he mourned, " and a good sixpenn'orth of wear and tear already. Inside the heel, outside the toe, or else viscery versery—that's where the cobbler looks for his emoluments. Iron tips ? No, I trust I shall never descend so low as that." He became aware of a fat dame smiling upon him close at hand, and his gloom lifted slightly at the prospect of a new listener. " Well," he continued, " 'tis a good observance of Jeremiah that it's not in man that walketh to direct his steps, and I reckon *he* knew what it was to wear out his sandals. After all, it's worse to be born with a wooden leg, and be obliged to squander one out of every pair of boots you buy."

"True," said the fat lady. "Dickon have got a yarn about that. 'Twas after a storm down west, and a great big packing-case come ashore to a cove, and the people in the cove, they got en hided up in a cavie unbeknown to the coast-guard, and when they come to break it open, lo and behold 'twas full of boots and shoes! So they went to sort 'em out and try 'em on, and, if I do live, those boots were left-foot boots every one! A brave disappointment for them all, as you may guess; but the worst was a man with a wooden leg, and who would have thought there was luck in the losing of legs?—

194

for 'twas his left leg was missing, and the
foot with it, of course, and if it had only
been the other one he'd 'a been set up
for life with boots. So the poor chap, he
went out before breakfast and hanged
himself in his own fish-cellar, and Dickon
says he'd 'a done the same thing himself
under the sarcumstances, if he'd been sure
there was somebody handy to cut him
down before any ser'ous damage was
done."

"Dickon?" said Albert. "Why, 'tis
Mrs. Varco, 'a b'lieve."

"That's of her," said the lady. "As
nat'ral as life, and twice as large, as Ann
Pedrick do say. And what's Albert
Hosken a-doing, all alone on one leg this
time of day?"

Albert overflowed. "Where's the fault
to? Who's to blame if you find me act-
ing like a pelican in the wilderness on a

day like this ?   I don't name no names,
but your daughter's the one ! "

" Dorinda ? " exclaimed Mrs Varco,
amused and incredulous.

" Dorinda, I daresay.   She hadn't the
politeness to inform me, nor I hadn't the
bad manners to ask.   Well, Dorinda Varco
it may be, and Dorinda Somewhat-or-
other it will be, no doubt, but never
Dorinda Hosken—make up your mind to
that.   I've been slighted before ; scores
of times I've been slighted, by her elders
and betters, too.   I've been scorned in
satin drawing-rooms by females twice her
age with more than one dead husband to
their credit.   I've been given the go-by in
favour of estate-agents by housekeepers in
titled families.   I've had solid oak doors
shut in my face by persons with copper-
plate visiting-cards of their own, leave
alone a trayful of other people's on the

hall table. And did I ever lose my self-respect? Not so much as a crumb of it! One trial is all I allow; I'm none of those you can turn off and on again like a beer-tap. No; once lost, I'm lost for ever, as many have found to their cost. Ah! there's sore hearts going around by the dozen this day, if the truth was known; and I'm sorry for your daughter—yes, I can say so much as that in my free, forgiving way—but she've only herself to blame; and as for the young chap, she won't get much consolation or credit out of *him*, by what I hear."

"What chap's that you're telling of?" asked Mrs. Varco sharply, her maternal instincts alarming her out of the dazed apathy to which Albert's conversation habitually reduced his listeners.

"With regard to waistcoats," replied Albert, "there's nothing secret or under-

hand about *me* ; *I*'ve no occasion to button
my coat up, nor my character neither.
I never damaged no female reputations,
by word or deed ; and as for costumery,
my wardrobe's open to inspection any
Sunday afternoon by respectable persons.
A man that owns the only trouser-press in
the parish—what does *he* care for your
slack-jawed young rips from Porthmellan
in their reach-me-down suits ? "

Mrs. Varco repressed a violent impulse
which bade her take him by the braces
and shake him as you shake a door that
jams when you are in a hurry to get at the
contents of the cupboard within.

" Albert," she said, " I beg of 'e, tell me
where my daughter's to, and who she's
with."

" Mind," he returned, " you can't hold
me responsible. I'm guaranteed against
all liability before witnesses, and I wash

my hands of her and him too. Laugh?
She can laugh if she've a mind to ; well
for her if 'tis the right side of her face.
I've set a whole parish meeting laughing
before now, and never made no joke
neither. Laugh?—ay, the crackling of
thorns under the pot ; and what do *they*
come to ? Dust and ashes ; and so for
her, if she an't careful. There's many a
maiden has laughed after tea and wept
before supper. Speaking personally, I'm
notorious for my morals, else her own
father wouldn't have trusted her with me.
But as for young Laity——"

"Harry Laity!" exclaimed Mrs. Varco.
"Our Dorinda gone off with Harry Laity?"

"Haven't I been telling 'e so all along?"
retorted Albert, righteously aggrieved.
"But there ! 'Tis all of a piece. I might
be a sparrer 'pon the house-top for all the
attention that's paid to me; and the more

I talk the less they listen. Don't wisdom
cry out in Hender Churchtown, same as
in Jerusalem ? Ay, that she do, and understanding putteth forth her voice in the
streets and places of concourse, bar-parlours
and cattle-markets. Better for her if she
saved her breath to cool her cocoa. Ah !
if King Solomon and Albert Hosken could
only get together for a quiet chat ! There'd
be some corroboration then, I reckon ; *he*
wouldn't scorn my words, simple bachelor
though I be, and him the completest
family man that ever was. Ah yes, and a
dressy man too, by all accounts. Him and
me 'ud coincide about neckties, I'll be
bound. 'Tis written in the Book of Kings
that he got the linen for his shirts from
Egypt, and I'd give something to know
how he found 'em for wearing value, by
comparison with Manchester goods. If it
wasn't for reversible cuffs———"

" La bless the man ! " cried Mrs. Varco, betwixt wrath and amusement ; " to hear 'e talk, 'tis like going to a jumble sale— cardboard texts, old clothes, everything but what you do want. Which way did they go ? "

" Well may you ask. But I'm roused at last. There's wrongs no man can bear. Old Harry's at his tricks with me at last ; I can feel him working powerful within. Darn it all ! There ! I've sworn an oath. Mother's great-uncle Silas once cussed the parson at a vestry-meeting, and they put him in the stocks for it—two hours after morning service with a crust of bread and a jug of water. He was the only man to distinguish himself in our family history, and 'twas feared the strain was lost. But blood will tell—be darned if it won't ! Ah ! Did 'e hear how easy it slipped out that time ? Who'll dare to scorn me now ?

And if I can swear, I can drink. Yes, I'm under conviction I can drink, and drink I will. Sorry to interrupt your conversation, my good woman, but I'm off to the inn to swig a noggin of peppermint with the other roysterers. If all goes well, my language won't be fit for female ears by the time dark sets in—'nation seize me if 'twill! There agin! Better and better! Off with 'e, Buck Albert, Devil-may-care Bert Hosken, on the ran-dan!"

With a creditable, if perilous, flourish of the silver-topped cane, with a less successful, but still praiseworthy, essay at a swaggering strut, Mr. Hosken took his new-found manhood off down the street. Released at last, Mrs. Varco went her way in search of her husband, for whom she had disquieting news.

VIII

MEANWHILE Dorinda and Harry Laity
went up the street in light converse.
Harry was agreeably satirical at the ex-
pense of various passers-by, and Dorinda
did not allow herself to be outdone in
vivacious criticism of this one's hat and
that one's gown. On such a basis an easy
intimacy is quickly established. At the
top of the street Harry casually proposed a
stroll up Love Lane to Trevellas Coombe.
Dorinda, ever so faintly alarmed, made
some demur, and suggested a return to
the madding crowd. Harry assented with
reassuring—and irritating—indifference,
and Dorinda changed her mind. Trevellas
Coombe was out of the question, but a
step or two up the lane was quite to her

fancy. So up the narrow lane they went, between high banks tapestried with penny-wort and creeping toadflax, and topped with a tangle of thorn and gorse and wild rose.

Steered by Harry, the conversation took a personal turn. His compliments were a bit extravagant, to be sure, but that only made them the easier to parry and make light of. And compliments were her due ; of that she had been thoroughly assured during the past few hours. The glib compliments merged by degrees into downright 'love-making ; and all at once, without his knowledge, Harry was addressing two distinct persons—a coy village maiden who blushed and giggled, fluttered and fenced, and a cool sensible young woman who stood oddly apart, reviewing the situation and finding it not altogether to her taste. What silly talk ! and what silly answers she was making ! Why was she walking alone in Love Lane with this common young fisherman of dubious reputation, for whom in truth she hadn't the least liking ? He was much too confident ; he talked as if he knew what he was saying without book. And what was he going to say next ?

What he said next was sillier than anything he had said before. It struck the village maiden dumb ; it resolved the sensible young woman on immediate action.

A turn of the lane brought into view a comparatively trim section of hedge, and in it a garden gate. Once before, years ago, Dorinda and a schoolfellow had crept up to that gate and peeped within for a sight of the mazed woman who lived 'pon kettle-broth and didn' consort with nobody. Their fearful curiosity had been rewarded

by a glimpse of a small figure in a faded
sunbonnet, bending over a border of blue
flowers ; then, as the figure straightened
itself and turned in their direction, they
had fled down the lane with tossing heels.
In the light of maturer information the
terror in the sunbonnet dwindled to Ann
Coad the harby-woman—a bit peculiar,
but no harm into her, the poor wisht
creature, and no wonder she "wasn't
exactly," as the saying went, living all
alone like she did, and the latch of her
gate not lifted sometimes for a week on
end, whether to go out or to let in. And
they did say she'd been in trouble years
ago and never got over it, though nobody
knowed the real rights of it all ; anyway
she hadn't a word to say to the men to
this day. A terrible fine musicianer, too,
or so they said else ; and pleasant-spoken
enough, if you could get mouth-speech of

her, and she didn' take and run at the
sight of 'e ; and her harby-tay was wonderful strong and comforting, sure enough.

So much Dorinda called to mind, and
determined to seek refuge within the
gate. She began to cast about for a
plausible excuse for quitting Harry's company. It would look silly to run off
without an ostensible reason, and it
mightn't be safe. Memory furnished an
inspiration.

" Oh ! " she cried, clapping her hand
to the back of her head. " My hair's
coming down ! "

A wavy tress fell on her shoulder for
corroboration. Harry's sleepy eyes kindled
at the sight of the charming disarray.

" Leave en bide as 'tis," he whispered.
" Us don't want to be stiff and proper
together, do us ? And you do look fifty
times so sweet and pretty like that." He

caught her waist. "The sweetest, prettiest little rogue of a maid I ever set eyes on. I don't hardly know what I'm saying or doing when I look upon 'e."

She strained away from him, with lips set against a scream.

"Silly little maid!" he said. "Ben't afraid of me, are 'e? Look now—we 'll go up by Trevellas Coombe, and I'll put your hair tidy myself. Such a handy chap as I am, you wouldn' believe. Nor I won't ask no payment, without 'tis one little kiss."

They were still a few yards from the gate. Dorinda steadied herself, and temporized.

"Poor wages, I reckon," she said.

"I don't dare ask no more," said Harry. "But I'll leave en to you. Such a kind-hearted little beauty as you are, you wouldn't be stingy with a chap, I know."

" That's as may be," she returned, and looked him full in the face with valiant coquetry. His face came nearer—the nasty grinning toad ! It was hard to keep it up, but she managed a natural little laugh as she flung her head back.

" No wages in advance ! " she said ; and then, with a pretty appealing timidity : " You'll take your arm away till we've passed the gate ? "

" 'Tis a lot to ask," said the gallant ; " but even if 'twas more, I couldn' say ' no ' to 'e for my soul. Mustn' shock old Mother Ann, must we ? "

His arm was withdrawn as they came level with the gate. The gate was ajar, offering no impediment to flight, and the faint long-drawn wail of a harmonium indicated that Ann Coad was at home. It was now or never ; yet for two paces she dallied with her resolution. Still

P 209

another Dorinda emerged—a wavering sceptic who asked herself what unbelievable story-book nonsense this might be : Dorinda Varco of Sunny Corner, treading the palpable ground of a commonplace St. Hender lane, and playing Lady Enid to the Sir Jasper of Harry Laity ! Silly, incredible stuff !

She felt his arm creeping round her again. A quick glance revealed his teeth gleaming in a hateful smile, and at the sight her whole body revolted and took the command of her brain. She whipped aside, doubled back, and in a moment was panting up the garden path behind the slammed gate.

The border of blue flowers was still there. What was Harry calling out to her ? And what dismal old tune was Ann Coad playing ? At the cottage door she collected her wits and turned. He was

at the gate, smiling. She felt sick and
faint ; as she looked, he dwindled and
was removed to a great distance.

" What's up with the dear little maid ? "
he called from afar.

She summoned strength to wave him
away.

" Don't be so foolish as you are," he
urged. " Can't think what I've done, that
you should treat me like this."

Keeping her eyes on him, she lifted her
hand to tap at the door.

" I'll wait, then," he said, no longer
smiling. " I'd wait for 'e till doomsday.
You'm worth it."

Still the slow music wailed within.
Dorinda knocked. The music hung
suspended on a chord, and sighed away to
nothingness. An initiate of the instrument
would have diagnosed a sudden cessation
of the motion of the bellows. Harry

opened the gate, and Dorinda, hurriedly trying the latch, discovered that the door was fastened inside. The arrested chord swelled on the air again, and the music went on through half a dozen quavering bars to its final cadence. Harry took a step or two up the path. Cold with terror, Dorinda was raising her fists for a frenzied assault on the door, when a bolt was drawn and the door opened a little way. Dorinda pushed in and shut the door behind her.

A small grey woman backed against the wall, stammering a frightened apology.

"Sorry to keep 'e waiting, but I got to finish the tune. If you break a tune, it hurt, if you understand. Like a soul cut off and set wandering before its time. Your — your hair's coming down."

Dorinda poured out an explanation.

The little woman listened with her eyes on the ground.

"I know," she said, when Dorinda was silent. "I haven' forgot. I could give 'e his words. But it take some sense and bravery to run away from 'em. Will 'e step inside, then?"

Dorinda went to the window. Harry had gone back to the gate, and was lounging over it in a comfortable attitude.

"He's waiting!" cried Dorinda, catching the little woman's arm. "He said he'd wait. Oh, what's to be done?"

Ann Coad flushed and stiffened. "The impident rogue!" she exclaimed. "With his elbows on my gate!" She apostrophized the unconscious Harry. "Aw, the great ugly rogue of 'e! Take thyself off o' my gate and go 'bout thy wicked business, will 'e?"

"Send him away!" cried Dorinda;

and for the second time on this momentous day she burst into hysterical tears.

"Don't take on so," fluttered Ann. "He can't touch 'e here. You can stay so long as you 've a mind to. We 'm quite safe. I'll slip the bolt again."

"Send him away!" sobbed Dorinda. "I can't bear it! Grinning over the gate there! Send him away!"

Ann's colour faded. "He won't go for the likes of me," she faltered.

Dorinda stamped her foot. "Send him away!" she repeated.

"I—I'm afraid," said Ann Coad. "I haven' faced a man, not since——"

"He won't touch *you!* Coward! Send him away! Send——"

"Aw, my dear life, what's to be done?" cried Ann, wringing her hands, while Dorinda laughed and wailed. "Don't 'e take on so, then! I'll do it, so I will.

214

He won't touch the likes of me, as you say. There; I'm going this minute."

Dorinda's frenzy died down; tired and listless, she watched the upshot from the window, as it might be some uninteresting show in which she had no personal concern. If there were any amusement left in the world, she might even have smiled at the sight of Ann Coad advancing on the adversary with the gestures of one who drives an intrusive cow from a cabbage-bed. Now the two were face to face at arm's-length, and things were being said by Ann in a shrill pipe, without evoking any reponse beyond an insolent smile from Harry. At last Harry leisurably detached himself from the gate, waved a mock-respectful farewell, and lounged out of sight. The dull show was over. Dorinda sank back in her chair and closed her eyes.

She opened them to find Ann Coad standing beside her, breathless and elate.

" Gone off like a lamb, my dear ! " she boasted. " Called en everything but a man, I did, and 'a couldn' take it up for his life. He 've larned his lesson, sure enough, the low, mean blaggurd. That's what I called en to his face. ' You low, mean blaggurd,' I said, ' just you take your great long arms off o' my gate, and go 'bout your dirty business,' I said ; and 'a couldn' find a word to answer me back— couldn' do nothing but just grizzle upon me like a chaney cat—looked some foolish, I can tell 'e. So I said—— But you 'm looking terrible wisht, my dear."

Dorinda wanly apologized. She couldn't think how she came to be so silly. And the way she had been behaving to her hostess——

" My dear, don't matter about that.

If it hadn' been for you, I'd have gone to my grave and never stood up to a bad man and told en what I thought of en. I'm glad I got the chance. But you 'm looking dreadful poorly. Must see what I can do for 'e."

From a cupboard she selected one from a great array of bottles, and poured some of the contents into a cup.

"Take and drink to that," she said. "There's ten different harbs into en, and one of 'em's borage—grand stuff for putting a heart into a person. 'I, borage, bring courage'—that's a good old observance. But you've got to take it with a spoon, and you've got to have faith—'tisn' no good else. Have 'e faith?"

"Yes, s'pose," said Dorinda, doubtfully inspecting the uninviting liquid.

"Here's a spoon, then. And while you're supping to it, I'll play a tune, if

you don't mind. I'm a bit shook up myself, and there's nothing like music for
settling the spirits."

Dorinda having politely expressed her
delighted acquiescence, Ann seated herself at the keys of a diminutive harmonium, and turned over the leaves of a
small oblong book, in which, as Dorinda
idly noted, the music was not printed, but
written off by hand.

"You won't hear none of these tunes
elsewhere," remarked Ann over her
shoulder ; "the real genuine old psalm
tunes, dead and gone to all the world these
many year. They don't make no such
tunes nowadays. Moody and Sankey
come up when I was a young maiden,
but I never took to 'em. You could fancy
yourself dancing to Moody and Sankey,
but you couldn' even tap your foot to
these. Real sacred music, sure enough."

She fluttered a leaf or two. "Dissolution, Plymouth Rock, Sprowston Lodge, Old Ninetieth—that's a grand old melody; I'll give 'e that."

The bellows creaked and wheezed, and Old Ninetieth went on its way at an appropriately patriarchal pace, with a senile pause for deliberation between each step. Sipping her draught, which fortunately didn't taste as bad as it looked, Dorinda delivered unfavourable judgment on the grand old melody. If this was the famed music of her forefathers, then give her Moody and Sankey for choice. Wisht melancholy stuff, to be sure! And old Ann, with her tightly drawn grey topknot swaying forth and back, her thin elbows jerking in and out, and her knees bobbing up and down—was there ever so queer a sight?

Old Ninetieth staggered his last step

219

and gave up the ghost. When Ann Coad turned about, her eyes were moist.

" Grand, edn' 'a ? " she said with a sniff. " If 'twasn' for music, I'd be a hard bitter woman, and no blame to me neither. But whenever I do feel that way, I've only got to set down and strike up, and my heart-strings are loosened to once . . . Shall I do up your hair for 'e ? "

Dorinda thought she could do it very well herself, if she had a looking-glass.

" My dear, if you'll believe me, I haven' got no such thing in the house. A bucket of water 've been more 'n enough for my vanities these twenty year and more. What do 'e think o' that, now ? "

Dorinda did what was obviously expected of her in the way of astonishment.

" A poor weed like me ! " said Ann with proud humility. " But I'd like to do

it up for 'e, if you don't mind. But
p'r'aps you'd rather I didn' touch 'e.
There's some maidens—well, they've the
right, s'pose——"

Dorinda immediately removed her hat
and turned her back, casually remarking
that the necessary hairpins would be easy
to find and safe to remove, as the structure had originally contained no fewer than
thirty-five of them.

"Thirty-five!" exclaimed her hostess,
gently handling the loosened tresses.
"Nor I don't wonder, though, so fine
and thick as 'tis. Mine never wadn' up
to much—thin and mean-coloured. But
I had a delicate shape, or so they said
else, and a skin to match a rose-leaf; and
so much the worse for me. Better-fit
I'd been one of these coarse lumpy ones."

There was a pause, and Dorinda felt
fingers nervously a-quiver in her hair.

DORINDA'S BIRTHDAY

"Don't look round, my dear," said Ann softly. Dorinda obediently kept still, and Ann began the story which no one in St. Hender had ever got the real rights of. There was nothing remarkable about it ; a country maiden does not attain the age of seventeen without hearing its counterpart a dozen times. A shabby stumbling little tale, from which all the colour had long since faded : but circumstances combined to impress it vividly on Dorinda's imagination. The light of recent events was lurid upon it. It was being told, not by a furtive school-fellow behind a raised desk, nor by an elderly gossip who parried whispered maternal remonstrances by declaring that the sooner the child know about such things the better, but by the pitiful heroine herself to a sister-woman—a real grown-up person whom she had chosen to be the exclusive recipient of her confidence. And in place of the visible looks and gestures which eke out a story, as it is ordinarily told, there came now and again the touch of unseen fingers that moved gently in her hair.

The story approached its end.

" The li'll cheeld didn' live to be reared. 'Twas a maid—so I was told. I didn' know nothing ; I was afflicted in my mind for the time. When I got better, they wanted me to stay at home, but I wouldn't. I went into sarvice up the country—same place for seven year ; thought a lot of me, they did. Then uncle died and left me a bit of money, and I came here. Been here ever since, doing my poor little bit o' good in the world with my harbs. I don't take no payment for my harbs ; shouldn' make much if I did. They ben't much in

vogue now." The fingers were busy
through a few silent moments. " Kept
myself quiet all the time, but you can't
stop things getting about. Don't matter
for that. 'Tisn' what people do think—
though, mind 'e, 'tis foolish to scorn what
people do think. 'Tis what *I* do think ;
'tis the shame for my own foolishness in
trusting the man. I never got over it,
nor I never shall. Sometimes I should
wake up of a night with it burning on
me. And now your hair's done, my dear,
so well as I can do it."

Standing up, and verifying the adjust-
ment of her tresses, Dorinda expressed
her opinion of the opposite sex in no
measured terms. They were all alike,
and she was resolved to have no truck
with them henceforth. Ann shook her
head, the ghost of a smile hovering on
her lips.

" Don't mind my talk," she said.
" I'm an old afflicted shadder of a person.
You 'm a lively, handsome young woman,
with plenty of sense and spirit, that just
wanted a lesson to put 'e to rights ; and
you've had it, cheap. You'll do very
well now, with all the brisk honest young
chaps in the place round 'e. And p'r'aps
you'd like to look round my garden before
you get back-along."

Reminded of the necessity of getting
back-along, Dorinda had an affrighting
vision of Harry lurking somewhere in
the lane.

" I could come with 'e to the end of
the lane," said Ann, divining her fears.
" If he's anywhere about, he won't dare
face *me* agin, you may be sure."

Before leaving the room in which she
had been sheltered from danger and entertained with music and medicine and

flattering confidences, Dorinda had a terrible mind to hug her queer hostess. But she allowed the opportunity to slip, and only the impulse can be placed to her credit.

Ann Coad led the way into the garden. As you go about the West Country, you will take note, if you are botanically inclined, of the neglected simples that everywhere linger in the neighbourhood of human habitations, perching on the walls of farmyards, struggling to maintain a foothold on rubbish-heaps. Their strange and vigorous faculties are fast passing into oblivion, but they are used to the company of man, and hang about him (as you like to think) in the hope of being taken into favour again. They have lost all taste—if the taste was ever theirs—for the wild disorderly life of the commons and hedge-rows.

226

They have seen better days; once they were looked up to and waited on in their ordered beds; but now their decayed gentility sits forlorn on dunghills, and the farmer's wife, returned from market with the latest thing in patent pills in her basket, steps from her trap and goes indoors without wasting a glance upon them.

In Ann Coad's garden these patient outcasts found safe refuge and honourable treatment. Here was that famous borage, whose very look inspires confidence; for who can behold that face of heavenly blue and doubt its transcendent virtue? Some indeed have conjectured that it was the sole ingredient of Helen's commended bowl, with which she expelled the melancholy from the breasts of her husband and Telemachus his guest. Here too was its cousin, the hardly less renowned bugloss;

tansy, the paschal herb, bitter but good ; mugwort, first and eldest of the Nine Mighty Herbs of our forefathers ; aromatic fever-few and camomile, for colds and calentures; agrimony and fennel, for purging the eyesight ; magical vervain, which the Druids gathered with a silver sickle ; steel-blue seaholm, whose candied roots dispel all pains, heal consumption, and restore the spirits ; and who knows how many more ! on whose various merits Ann discoursed at length, while Dorinda did her best to display an intelligent interest in what she mentally stigmatized as a parcel of old weeds. Ann was a good old soul, and Dorinda was immensely grateful to her ; but, after all, this was Hender Feast-day, and the moments were too precious to squander in listening to dull quotations from anybody bearing such an absurd name as Culpepper.

Near the gate Ann suddenly broke off to listen.

"Somebody's coming up the lane," she said. "You keep behind me while I look."

Cautiously reconnoitring, she announced the approach of two people, an old man and a boy. Dorinda ventured to peep, and at once laughed a recognition of Charles Edward and his uncle Lazarus. Explaining to Ann that these were friends who would see her safely back, she thanked her prettily for her kindness, and added, as in duty bound, that she would come and see her again some time.

Ann was already shrinking back into the solitary self from which Dorinda's dramatic advent had stirred her. "I don't look for that," she said, shaking her head, "nor I don't wish it neither, if you don't mind my saying so—without you should

be wanting harbs. P'r'aps we shouldn'
get on so well another time. I ben't
going to risk it. I shall be thinking a
brave lot about the pretty face of 'e, but
I'm bound to go on keeping to myself.
So good-bye, and wish 'e well."

She faded up the path. Dorinda
looked after her for a moment, vexed and
puzzled ; then with a shrug she shut the
gate on Ann Coad, and went smiling
down the lane to meet her friends.

" What be a-doën up 'ere-along, you ? "
she sang, in the rustic drawl which she
and Charlie sometimes affected, for drol-
lery, and to set off the refinement of their
normal accents.

Mr. Roscorla's architectural smile was
exhibited in all its massive grandeur,
quite dwarfing Charles Edward's feebler
effort.

" Come to fetch 'e," said the latter.

" Awful good of 'e, I'm sure ! " exclaimed Dorinda, tossing her head ; and along the lane they went, the aged ox and the callow calf on either side, the sprightly young heifer in the middle. If you have ever properly made the acquaintance of a young Alderney heifer—a little patience and a handful of salt will do the trick—you will accept the trope with enthusiasm.

" What's everybody doing without me ? " asked Dorinda.

" Your father's searching for 'e down-along, and your mother's waiting for news of 'e in the churchyard, and aunt's staying by her—to cheer her up, *she* says."

" My life, what a fuss ! Can take care of myself, s'pose."

Charles Edward grinned uneasily, and returned no answer.

" And what's Hubert doing ? *He* isn't searching around too, surely ? "

" Hubert was walking with Laura Pengelly, last I see him," replied Charlie.

" Oh ! " said Dorinda, biting her lip. " Well, the poor chap must have somebody," she conceded. " And what have 'e done with May Tregilgas ? Oh, Charlie ! *I* saw you ! And how my poor old heart did thump ! "

" Don't want to hear nothing about May Tregilgas," said Charlie with some heat.

" Slighted again ? " laughed Dorinda.

Charlie nodded. " These women ! " he ejaculated.

" Poor Charlie ! 'Twill be a lesson to 'e. We ben't to be trusted, that's certain. But, Charlie, how come you to be looking for me up here ? "

" That was uncle," explained Charlie.

" I wanted to keep along the road, but he said he reckoned you'd gone up Love Lane."

" Oh, he did, did he ? " Dorinda turned on Mr. Roscorla, placidly plodding at her elbow. " What's the meaning of this ? " she severely inquired. " How should you reckon I'd gone up Love Lane, I'd like to know ? "

The muscles at the outer corner of Mr. Roscorla's inner eye suffered a slow and painful contraction.

" I was a frolicsome young spark once," he said.

IX

In the deserted churchyard a low-spirited trio of staid folk started into animation at the approach of Dorinda and her escort. Advancing a step in front of his wife and Miss Roscorla, Mr. Varco set a hand on each of his daughter's shoulders, and closely scanned her face. Dorinda's colour deepened to scarlet, but her eyes met the scrutiny bravely enough.

"All right, mother!" he exclaimed. "Just a bit of a smut, side of her nose, but that's soon got rids of." The crimson table-cloth was gravely brought into requisition. "There; now go and kiss your ma, like the good clane maid you are."

" But there wadn' no smut that I could see," cried Miss Roscorla.

" Hush ! " breathed Mrs. Varco with a composite laugh and sigh, as Dorinda emerged from her capacious embrace. " 'Tis only one of Dickon's quips."

" I can take up a quip so quick as anybody," said Miss Roscorla. " But I don't see the fun of saying there's a smut when there an't no such thing. If that's the way to concoct a quip, 'tis as easy as lying, and terrible like it too. But I'm glad you 'm back again safe and sound, Dorinda, and I hope 'twill be a warning to 'e after the anxious time we've had about 'e, knowing how easy 'tis for a young maiden to be led astray———"

We give Miss Roscorla all credit for the best intentions, but isn't she taking a little too much upon herself ? There

was a general stir in Dorinda's defence.
Mrs. Varco nudged her officious friend,
and whispered, " Hush then, will 'e ? "
quite sharply ; Mr. Roscorla cleared
his throat with surprising alacrity ;
Charles Edward tugged viciously at his
own hair ; and Dickon raised his voice
in a loud reminder that the snake-walk
was to begin at eight o'clock, and that
it was time to be getting round to the
meadow if folk didn't want to miss the
great fun of all. Miss Roscorla bated
her breath to a murmured justification
of words in due season, and the party
moved off, Dorinda walking ahead with
her father, her faithful knight and squire
following next, and the elder ladies bringing up the rear.

Possessed by the setting sun, the glebe
meadow was a great shining hall of light,
across which gigantic shadows stalked,

with small mortals attached to them.
In the centre stood a man with a flag.
Behind him, two by two in processional
order, were ranged the Harmonious Rechabites, from the shrill cornets to the
gruff euphoniums. Then came the big
drum, with a little drummer clinging to
it like an ant on a gooseberry, and thereafter a train of couples, brief at present,
but lengthening every moment.

Dorinda was not looking out for anybody in particular, but she could not help
noticing somebody, and Laura Pengelly
with him, sure enough, going across the
meadow to take their places. Arm-acrook,
too ; but that didn't mean anything ;
you had to go arm-acrook in the snake-
walk. Laura was hanging on his arm as
if she belonged there permanently ; but
that again didn't mean much ; Laura
would do the same by anything in

237

trousers, when the opportunity afforded. And it didn't matter, anyhow; and anyhow she had no right to complain of Hubert's behaviour, or Laura's, or anybody's. And maybe, if it came to a tug of war, she might prove a match for any of your freckled, sandy-haired St. Hender dumplings. Meanwhile, whether she deserved it or not, it was not altogether pleasant to be left out of the great fun of all for lack of an escort.

"Come along, daddy," she said tapping her foot.

Mr. Varco affected amazement. "Don't 'e do anything so desperate as that!" he exclaimed. "Go snake-walking with your own father, when there's staid bachelors a-hovering around with their arms all ready crooked for 'e! Besides, your ma 'ud be jealous if I didn't ask *her*."

"Now, Dickon!" protested Mrs. Varco.

"When my breathing wouldn' carr' me once round, as you do very well know ! If you can call it breathing, when 'tidn' no more than two gasps and a guggle all the while."

"Then I'm free to foller my own heart," said her husband, offering his arm with insinuating gallantry to Miss Roscola. At the same moment Dorinda felt the pressure of something hard against her side, and discovered it to be the point of an elbow. If anything I have said has led you to infer that Mr. Roscorla was slow to take a hint, let that saying be cancelled and obliterated from your memory. There he stood, brown and knotty and emotionless as Lord Derby himself, with one crooked branch rigidly extended for the maid to swing on. The silent invitation was not to be resisted.

"We'll keep together so close as we

can," said Mr. Roscorla's ever-vigilant sister, taking Dickon's arm.

"So close as we can," echoed Dickon with a wink. "And everybody to meet outside the inn at nine o'clock."

The couples were now hurrying up thick and fast, and the place which Dorinda and her partner took in the tail of the procession was soon a place well in the middle. Hubert and Laura were a little way in front; Mr. Varco and Miss Roscorla, thanks to some malicious manœuvre on the part of the former, were an indistinguishable distance in the rear. Presently the influx slackened and ceased. The guardian of the flag jerked it out of the ground, and lifted it on high; the Harmonious Rechabites shook the last drops of accumulated moisture from their instruments and raised them to their mouths; the little big-drummer set the pace with

three resounding thwacks ; the two pretty
girls next behind him shrieked with
laughter as they ducked to avoid the
backward rebounding drumsticks; and to
the inspiring strains of the March in
Scipio the snake-walk began.

I have always carefully refrained from
inquiring into the antecedents of the St.
Hender snake-walk, fearing to be told that
it is a recent introduction, and, in fact, a
mere glorification of the childish game
of follow-my-leader. By remaining in
resolute ignorance on this point, I am at
liberty to plunge with a free conscience in
search of its origin among the mists of the
conveniently dim Druidic past, and to
discourse as learnedly as I please of mystic
tribal dances and the cult of the Sacred
Serpent. When the man with the flag
begins by fetching a wide compass, until
he treads on the heels of the last of his

R   241

followers, I confidently infer a traditional representation of the ancient symbol of eternity—the snake swallowing its own tail. When, suddenly swerving aside, he heads the way up the field in a series of subtle convolutions, "and of his tortuous train Curls many a wanton wreath," it is easy to discern a curious figuring forth of the progress of creation out of that endless ring into the labyrinthine errors of Time. And if the chattering and laughing performers remain unconscious of the deep significance of their proceedings, and are content to enjoy the mere delight of stepping in time to a rhythmic tune, and of surrendering their volition for the nonce to the irresponsible guidance of a red-faced man with a flag, yet the philosophic observer can still admire the wisdom of their feet, and complacently reflect that snake-walking, like all forms of the dance,

242

DORINDA'S BIRTHDAY

" . . . is an exercise,
Not only shows the mover's wit,
But maketh the beholder wise,
As he hath power to rise to it."

The mazy evolutions had endured for
a full quarter of an hour; one or two
elderly faint-hearts had dropped out, and
several of the younger folk had attained a
painfully exact knowledge of the spot
where the new shoe pinched; when one of
the leading bandsmen, snatching the cornet
from his lips in the middle of a bar,
warned the fugleman that he and his
mates had pretty well blowed their souls
away, and that further expenditure of
breath was not to be looked for at five
shillings a man. The fugleman nodded,
and prepared for the final manœuvre by
shaping a straight course for his starting-
point in the middle of the field. Here he
began what appeared at first to be the

primary evolution over again ; but before the circle was joined, a slight change of direction converted it into an inward-winding spiral. A shout from the knowing ones gave warning to all of the imminent climax. Tighter and tighter were drawn the coils, slower and slower grew the pace, until, amid much laughter and shrieks not a few, the leader lifted his flag at arm's length and stood calmly triumphant in the centre of a huddled mass of breathless humanity. I am unable to decide precisely what esoteric interpretation to attach to this ending, unless it be a dark hint of chaos as the final goal of the universe, but at any rate I can assure you that it is indubitably the great fun of all.

Some moments earlier, Dorinda had inadvertently slipped her hand from Mr. Roscorla's arm, and the difference in their specific gravities had quickly drifted them asunder. The band had still some bars to play, and Dorinda found herself tightly wedged against a wall of resounding brass, with a bombardon bellowing furiously in her ear, while a trombone with no room for horizontal extension was making sharp lunges in the direction of her toes. And close at hand, almost near enough to touch, was Hubert, with Laura still firmly attached. Their eyes met in a grave look.

The music ceased, with the effect of a cosmic catastrophe. After a solid fifteen minutes of the March in *Scipio*, you are inclined to believe that it was composed for the use of the morning stars at the beginning of all things, and had been going on ever since. When Dorinda's ears recovered their faculties, they became aware of the player of the bombardon offering apologies for hooting and bleating in her face to such an unmannerly extent.

245

Duty had to be done, and occasions like
this called for coarse playing ; but when
he had the chance he could put it in as
tender and sweet as boiled turnips. Wasn't
that so, Arthur ?

Arthur, pushing home the slide of his
trombone, confirmed the bombardon's
statement, and remarked further that join-
ing a band put an excessive strain on a
teetotaler's convictions, but he supposed
it would have to be ginger ale as usual.
And if the young lady would like to share
something of the sort with two respectable
young men from the china-clay district,
who had finished up their job for the day,
and had a solid hour to wait for the brake
to start, and didn't possess a single female
acquaintance in this benighted spot, why
then——

The bombardon reproved his too san-
guine colleague. Did Arthur expect such

dazzling luck at this time of day? Couldn't
he see that the young lady was looking
out for a friend, whose shoes any man
might account himself fortunate to wear?
And where was his discrimination? The
young lady was obviously not the sort to
pick up with chance strangers, however
respectable. Dorinda was entreated to
believe that Arthur was constitutionally
the most retiring of men; but the effect
of gold braid on a man's character was
notorious.

Arthur agreed. The wearing of a
uniform would give confidence to a rabbit.
And did Dorinda happen to know the
name of that smart young woman over
yonder with the tall young fellow in tow?
A tidy piece, sure enough; and of a
coming-on disposition, if his knowledge
of the sex went for anything. He didn't
want to spoil sport, but judging by the

looks she was casting in his direction, it
would be an easy job to get her to cut the
tow-line.

Laura and Hubert, after moving a few
yards away with the dispersing crowd, had
come to a standstill, obviously on Laura's
initiative ; and it was she who was now
making play with those bold eyes of hers
for the benefit of the susceptible trombone,
who began forthwith to chirrup and murmur seductive endearments under his
breath. Dorinda could not help tittering
at his ridiculous behaviour, and apparently
the titter decided Laura, who came straight
towards them, leaving Hubert to follow as
he pleased. The bombardon opined that
the gold braid had done the trick once
more, and warned Arthur that it was his
firm intention to stand by him to the
end.

Laura accosted Dorinda, sweetly won-

dering how she had contrived to get that
nasty stain on her new frock, and hoping
she was having a proper good time. For
her own part, she was as dull as a dead
duck in a mud-pool. A resentful glance
drove the remark home into Hubert's
bosom.

The trombone gallantly interposed. It
was shameful that a shadow of depression
should rest on one so fair. He ventured
to suggest a remedy. Five was generally
considered an awkward number to deal
with on occasions like this, but it was
precisely on occasions like this that he and
his friend the bombardon counted as one,
and after all the young lady had two arms
to dispose of. He awaited her opinion on
the subject.

Laura's opinion, mitigated in its sever-
ity by a brilliant smile, was to the effect
that the impudence of some people was

unparalleled in her experience ; and what did the trombone take her for ?

The trombone, it appeared, took her for one whose sense was on a level with her charm, and who would therefore realize at once that, with the brake starting for home at nine-thirty sharp, two respectable young men from the china-clay district had no time to waste in dilly-dallying. " Fall in " was therefore the word.

Laura made the witty, if obvious, retort that she would fall out with somebody pretty and quick if he didn't behave ; and then, without more ado preparing to depart with a uniform on either side, she leaned back to address Dorinda with a sugared smile.

" You 'm welcome to my leavings once more," she whispered.

The three made off in close marching order, leaving a self-conscious and irresolute couple to dawdle in their wake. Less than three hours had elapsed since their dramatic severance at the festal board ; but for Dorinda, at any rate, that brief period had been so thronged with ripening incident and experience that she looked back to her innocent flirtation over the teacups as to a remote happening of her vanished childhood. Yet how grown-up she had felt at the time ! And she could not help wondering whether Hubert had heard Laura's last words, and if he had, what he would make of them. Perhaps he knew something already ; evidently Laura did— the spiteful cat ! It was useless to pretend she didn't care ; she did care very much, but not in any silly courting sort of way. She only wanted to be on pleasant, friendly terms with all the world, excepting Laura, of course, but certainly including the big boy who lived next door at Sunny Corner.

All the same she wasn't going to make the first advance.

As for Hubert, he had Laura on his conscience, though the burden was not very heavy. When a young man is mooning idly about, nursing a sore place or two, and a lively and well-looking young woman accosts him with a direct challenge, he is to be commended rather than blamed for rising to the occasion ; all the more so if he doesn't care twopence for the said young woman. Still, the rules of the game permitted and even enjoined Dorinda to take offence at his defection. Anyhow, *he* wasn't going to make the first advance.

They walked on in silence, each a little afraid of the other. As for the eternal separation which had lately been decreed against them, I don't believe it entered the minds of either, except to be dismissed as a negligible and impertinent folly.

They had gone half-way to the entrance of the meadow, when they both decided simultaneously that this was too foolish to be permitted to continue. Two furtive glances were caught together, two nervous smiles encouraged each other into confidence, two innocent hands came into contact and interlocked, and the world was reconstituted in the same shape as when it had been shattered by an angry old man.

I have read somewhere that the custom of man and maid going arm-acrook is quite a modern innovation, and I have since searched in vain for any mention of it in the old writers. To take but one instance, and that the earliest of all, it was hand in hand, as Milton testifies, that Adam and Eve went to their bower ; and hand in hand again they took their solitary way out of Paradise. And even if Milton's

authority on antediluvian etiquette be
questioned, his statement is a sufficient
indication, I think, that he, the seven-
teenth-century citizen of London, never
in his life walked arm in arm with Mary
Powell. On the comparative merits of
the two methods much might be said.
Both are good ; though for snugness no
doubt the linked elbows carry the day.
But the other is certainly the more delicate, flexible and sensitive form of attach-
ment. Children, to whom we must go to
learn the unperverted language of the affec-
tions, recognize no intermediate between
hand in hand and arm about neck ; and a
fairly close observation of the ways of
married folk has taught me that husband and wife may go arm in arm for fifty
reasons, of which not the least is mere
habit, but that when you see husband
and wife walking hand in hand, you may

safely ignore other evidence—wrinkles, grey hairs and all—and conclude that they are sweethearts still.

Hand in hand went Dorinda and Hubert on their way, swinging their arms a little to emphasize the fraternal nature of the bond between them. Whether there was any ultra-fraternal variation in the pressure of their fingers, is nobody's affair ; nor were the few words that passed between them of sufficient importance, even to themselves, for the chronicler to notice. As they wandered along, quietly and soberly enjoying each other's company, their ears were suddenly assailed with the vast uproar of a mechanical organ, to which the utmost efforts of the Harmonious Rechabites were but a soothing lullaby. Sucked in by the overwhelming sound, like straws on the brink of Niagara, they drifted round a corner into a by-street. Here, on a piece of roadside waste, stood the merry-go-round, or, as it particularized itself in great gilt letters: " Baragwanath's Galloping Horses, the Pride of the Duchy," affronting the dying day with an insolent flare of naphtha lamps, and pouring forth from its glittering axis a florid and voluble version of the most blatant of rag-time melodies. The cavalcade was at that moment in full career, and by some marvel of mechanics each one of every well-matched pair of steeds soared and sank alternately with its companion. If the Vicar had been standing by, he would certainly have quoted from the Mantuan—

" Jamque humiles jamque elati sublime videntur
  Aera per vacuam ferri atque adsurgere in auras."

It was pretty to watch the riders as they flashed past, the maidens sitting side-long in attitudes of studied elegance, the youths easily astraddle, not unconscious of witching the world with wooden horsemanship. Most were allowing their looks to wander among the earth-fettered bystanders, with that indifferent superiority which we have all felt when our express train glides past the crowded suburban platform. But there were couples who had no eyes save for each other, and it was the oddest sight to see their intent faces go up and down as youth and maiden rose and fell in turn. It was fascinating, too, to observe the death-tempting progress of the dark gipsy youth who swung about the dizzy circle, collecting twopences, as a monkey might collect nuts in a windy tree-top.

The whirling circle slowed and stopped; the music ceased a moment later, and you heard, high up in a neighbouring tree, the sweet wistful note of a redbreast, who had

s

all the while been straining his throat over his evening hymn in valiant emulation of the steam monster below. You guessed his triumph at having sung his rival down at last. But the monster only awaited the turning of a crank, and that thin trickle of pure sound was swallowed up in a renewed tempest of polyphony. This time it was an indelicately languorous waltz of the approved modern pattern. In your mind's eye you saw a ball-room in Brobdingnag, where Cormoran and Blunderbore, broad-acred with shirt-fronts, leered on buxom giantesses with Alpine shoulders, and thundered sweet nothings in their ears as they steered them over the quaking floor.

Dorinda and Hubert had already chosen and mounted their steeds——a piebald and a roan. A dolorous and thrilling whistle sounded ; the ground slid away from beneath them, slowly and then faster. Within a single revolution they found themselves alone together in a still, fairy region, outside and above the wildly spinning earth and the men and trees that span with it in a senseless blur. Their magic steeds rocked gently beneath them, motionless else ; a great rushing wind was in their faces—surely the same that blew out of Eden after the Fall, scattering the seeds of life over the waiting world ; all about them surged in a mighty tide the music of the spheres, which is so loud and omnipresent that it cannot be heard at all by earth-borne folk.

After a while, Dorinda made the experiment of shutting her eyes, the better to taste the rapture of the moment Feeling giddy at once, she opened them again on the youth beside her ; and behold, it was the same wonderful youth she had seen in the ringing-chamber. He stooped towards her, whispering something that was manifestly of supreme importance, could she but hear it across the chiming of the spheres. Her brows signalled for a repetition. He reddened, hesitated, and ventured once more—

" Dear girl ! "

" Oh ! " said Dorinda, and frowned, and instantly repented of her frown as belonging to the idiot conventions of the distant earth, and stooped forward in her turn, and sweetly breathed the parallel stave of the antiphony—

" Dear boy ! "

Then a dirty hand was thrust before them, and a rude Egyptian ape sarcastically urged his pretty love-birds to hurry up with their twopences.

X

At half-past eight Mr. and Mrs. Varco
paused outside the door of the inn. He
had some business to transact inside,
which, after the way of inn-business, might
take him five minutes and might take him
half an hour, and she was reckoning to go
up to Mrs. Pedrick's again, to glean any
whips and straws of news that might have
been wafted through that hospitable door
during the past hour or two. Mr. Varco
let his wit play briefly round a satirical
picture of the main street of St. Hender,
with its serried array of scandal-traps
gaping wide all day, year in, year out;
and they were just parting, when the inn-
door was flung open, and Albert Hosken
projected himself therefrom in some

disorder. Catching sight of Mrs. Varco, he brought himself up with a jerk, and splashed over in speech.

" No good, ma'am—no good at all. Nothing but a flash in the pan. I've tried peppermint and port-wine nagus ; I've tried trolling a randy stave ; and not so much as a glimp' of Old Harry's tail have I catched again. Don't think me worth his trouble, s'pose, the proud old rip ! To be slighted by the devil—'tis the last straw in the camel's eye. I'll go home to bed."

Abruptly he flung away, and Mr. and Mrs. Varco were unexpectedly free to depart on their errands. We follow the former, who, entering the inn, paused listening for a moment at the door of the farmers' parlour, nodded to himself, and passed on into the tap room, where his appearance was hailed with a shout of welcome. Dickon's visits to the inn were of the rarest, and were treasured accordingly. Sitting down, he beckoned to Sally the brisk handmaid, and gave his modest order.

"Mr. Barron in yonder?" he asked, indicating the parlour.

"Yes, Mr. Varco. Been here this hour and more."

"What's he taking?"

"Sixpenny mostly, Mr. Varco. Rum now and agin."

"H'm!" Dickon reflected. "Talking much?"

"Not till just now. He come in in a fine poor temper—nothing to say to nobody. But now he's laying down the law pretty and loud."

"Hat over his eyes?"

Sally nodded shrewdly.

"Leave me know when it get back of his head, will 'e?"

263

Sally made a mental calculation. In the sober world outside she passed for something of a simpleton, but of her own moist sphere she had a specialist's knowledge, and could gauge the symptoms of the mounting of good liquor as easily as you or I can read a barometer.

"That 'll be when he's finished up his next glass," she said. "He's slow to start, but quick to get on. 'Bout nine o'clock, I reckon."

"Nine o'clock 'll be just right for me," said Dickon; and putting Nick Barron out of his head for the time, he turned to the expectant company and launched his first side-splitting jest.

At three minutes to nine, Sally touched his shoulder and pantomimed the awaited news.

"Right," quoth Dickon, getting up. The revellers who sought to detain him

were left to make what they could of
the information that he was going to
pick a ripe apple, front of the house.
Passing forward, he opened the parlour
door.

Temperance advocates have so many
powerful arguments at their command,
that they can surely afford to present a
case like Mr. Barron's to their opponents.
For six days in the week, and for all but
a brief portion of the seventh, he was as
you have seen him, a man of sterling
worth and undoubted integrity, but some-
what crabbed and crotchety, dangerously
apt to take offence, and invincibly suspicious of hidden roguery everywhere—
in short, a terrible hard man to get on
with. But from nine o'clock onwards on
Saturdays and on such festal nights as
this, he blossomed under the ministrations
of Sally into the most robustly genial of

mortals, good-humoured even to boister-
ousness, and unsuspecting and tractable as
a child. In this condition, who would
venture to call him anything but the
better for drink ? Who might not indulge
the generous thought that this perhaps
was the real Nick Barron, and the other
but an inessential husk, woven about him
by sour-faced circumstance, and only to
be dissolved in malt liquor ?

Dickon's purpose was achieved as soon
as he was seen. Out of his seat against
the opposite wall, from which his hat
was fending his nape, Nicky sprung forward with a welcoming roar.

"Aha, Dickon Varco! Dickon the
quipster, come to make it up with his old
chum over a friendly glass ! Shake hands,
then, and name your tipple."

The hand-shake was cordially exchanged,
but Dickon excused himself from the

266

tipple, reckoning he had had enough to float him home."

"Hear that!" shouted his friend to the company. "That's good. 'Enough to float me home'—capital, sure enough! Three cheers for Dickon Varco, the celebrated joker! Pitch us another joke now, Dickon."

Dickon did not flatter himself that the laugh which went round was a tribute to his wit. There are two sore trials with which an accepted humorist is liable at any time to be confronted. The one is when—to take the stock instance—his request for the mustard sets the table rocking, the other when an exhibition of his powers is importunately demanded. The one and the other befalling Dickon in quick succession left him unperturbed. His one business now was to lure his friend from his liquor while yet the jovial mood was on him, and this he did with a neat turn of the wrist.

" The best joke of all's outside," he said, mysteriously beckoning. At once Mr. Barron laid his finger as mysteriously to his nose, and followed Dickon out of the parlour like a lamb.

Outside in the gathering twilight he peered about, swaying a little, and urgently demanding the instant production of the joke. Whether Dickon's powers of jocular inspiration would have proved equal to the emergency I cannot say ; for at that moment fortune played into his hand. A young couple, affectionately interlaced, strolled out of the dusk and stood gazing into the lighted window of the shop hard by.

" Look," whispered Dickon. " There 'tis."

Nicky stared. " How ? My boy and

268

your maid, edn' 'a ?   Where the joke in
that ? "

" Your boy and my maid, and the
joke's with you.   Haven't forgot, have
'e ?   What business they got with one
another's waistes this side Jedgment
Day ?   Now then, starn parent, for'ard
with 'e, and frighten them out of their
lives."

Nicky subdued a chuckle.   " Dickon
the quipster !   Joke's with me, sure
enough.   None of your sly winking
behind my back, then."

He cautiously advanced to the rear of
the unsuspecting pair.

" Oho there ! " he rumbled threaten-
ingly.   They sprang apart and turned.   He
eyed them grimly up and down.   " And
what are you two doing together, I'd like
to know ? "

There was an interval of downcast

silence. Then the maiden lifted roguish
eyes on Nicky and Dickon, and said with
soft impudence—

" Well, if it come to that, what are
you two doing together, I'd like to
know ? "

Shaking with laughter, Nick Barron
slapped his old chum's shoulder.

" Hear that, Dickon ? The joke's with
the maid after all. Catched us out fair !
Rolled us over, so clean as a smelt ! Best
joke of all, sure enough ! "

" Chip of the old block," said the other
senior with quiet pride. " And here come
the Roscorlas. Time to be getting on
backwards. You coming too ? "

Mr. Barron was certainly coming too.
It was Sunny Corner against all the inn-
parlours in the world for wit and good
company. From Sunny Corner had
proceeded the best joke of all, which
it would take till bedtime to savour

properly. Let Lazarus Roscorla judge
for himself.

A cloudy recapitulation of all the events
necessary to the comprehension of the
joke of jokes occupied Mr. Roscorla's pas-
sive ear all the way to Mrs. Pedrick's
door. Here the good-humoured and
rather noisy company filled the kitchen
and partook of just a morsel of cake all
round, to stay their stomachs against
supper. Once more Mrs. Pedrick inquired of the fitty maid whether she had
found a chap yet, and once more Dorinda
replied that maybe she had and maybe
she hadn't. Hubert looked rather solemn
and sheepish at the sally, which only
heightened the excellence of its reception
by the rest. Then farewells were said,
Mrs. Varco was uprooted from her chair,
and the homeward journey was begun in
good earnest.

The sky behind them was still bright

with rose-red and apple-green ; a belated
cuckoo was calling ; the rising incense of
the hedges mingled agreeably with the
more pungent fumes of Mr. Varco's pipe.
At the crest of the hill that shelters Sunny
Corner they had a glimpse of a calm
marmoreal sea, all milky white, with a
wonderful great orange. disc just mounting above it. Everybody agreed that the
moon was looking handsome to-night,
and Dorinda and Hubert lingered to pay
her majesty a less perfunctory tribute.
When they followed down the hill, the
others were a turn of the road ahead, and
Mr. Barron's laughter was mellow in the
distance. They crossed the stream, and
passed the forge, and entered the gate.
Under the benignant shelter of Lord
Derby they came to a stand, listening to a
colloquy that was going on before the
doors of Sunny Corner.

" Well, missus, how feeling now ? "
That was Mr. Barron, to be pictured
wide-balanced on careful legs, as with
upturned face he addressed his wife in her
lonely eyrie.

" Better, Nicholas," came the answer.
" But what's my better put en agin
other people's worse ? Are 'e sober,
Nicholas ? "

" Not by a long chalk, my dear," was
the jovial reply.

" Then you'll sleep on the sofa, if you
plaise.   Where's Hubert ? "

" Hubert's coming on behind.   With
Dorinda."

" With Dorinda ?   Ah—h'm ! "   Mrs.
Barron appeared to be digesting the
information.   " Well, he might do worse,
I will say that for her."

Mrs. Varco's voice was raised, with
some emphasis and a shade of acrimony :

" And *she* might do worse, I will say that for *him*."

Mr. Varco chimed in : " Trust the women for settling these kind of jobs off-hand. Shall we call 'em in and give 'em our j'int blessings ? "

" Hush, Dickon ! They'll hear 'e. They'm just behind."

Confused murmurs followed. Then Miss Roscorla was heard, clear and sharp.

" Now then, Lazarus ! If 'tis worth the saying, say it, and don't keep us waiting."

" Husband-high, neighbours ! " Thus Mr. Roscorla in husky triumph. " Didn' I say so ? And when a maid's husband-high——"

Mr. Varco's voice interrupted him, sober and serious, purged of all raillery : " Well, well, uncle, time enough yet for what time will show. But if 'a should

be so some day, Sunny Corner couldn'
wish to hear better news. And there's
my two grandf'ers making up their
totalish old minds for half-past nine.
Worky-day again to-morrow, my friends.
Good-night all."

Good-nights were chorused, and closing
doors set silence free among the apple-
trees. Dorinda and Hubert looked at each
other with enormous solemnity.

THE END

Richard Clay & Sons, Ltd., London and Bungay.

CPSIA information can be obtained at www.ICGtesting.com
Printed in the USA
BVOW05s1053250214

345948BV00017B/701/P